The I ♥ TRADER JOE'S® COLLEGE Cookbook

150 Cheap-and-Easy Gourmet Recipes

Andrea Lynn

ULYSSES PRESS

Published by
Ulysses Press
P.O. Box 3440
Berkeley, CA 94703
www.ulyssespress.com

ISBN: 978-1-56975-935-6
Library of Congress Catalog Number 2011922515

Printed in the United States by Versa Press

10 9 8 7

Acquisitions Editor: Keith Riegert
Managing Editor: Claire Chun
Editors: Lauren Harrison, Leslie Evans
Proofreader: Elyce Petker
Design and layout: what!design @ whatweb.com
Cover photos: pizza, pulled pork sandwich, fajitas, pasta and caramel popcorn
    © www.judiswinksphotography.com; bell peppers © Alexey Smirnov/shutterstock.com;
    kitchen utensil © Artistic Endeavor/fotolia.com; pasta © Peter Bernik/shutterstock.com;
    beer © Doris Rich/shutterstock.com; math class doodle © dddb/istockphoto.com;
    pizza illustration © marinamik/fotolia.com
Food stylist for pictured recipes: Anna Hartman-Kenzler
Interior photos: see page 156

TABLE OF CONTENTS

ACKNOWLEDGMENTS

Thank you to all my friends and family who lent tons of encouragement—along with their stomachs to taste all the food—while I wrote the cookbook. Also, a big thanks to the ever-helpful staff at the NYC Trader Joe's locations.

INTRODUCTION

Trader Joe's is a mecca of affordable, good-quality, delicious food—perfect for the college student who wants more than just cafeteria meals. With a little creativity and this cookbook in hand, you can transform Trader Joe's ingredients into a mouth-watering array of nibbles and meals.

The purpose of this cookbook is to highlight basic recipes with step-by-step instructions, utilizing the wonder that is Trader Joe's. Take it from someone who's sampled every ingredient the company makes: From packaged snacks to fresh veggies to frozen meals, there's a reason why the chain is so popular—the food is unique and tasty, and they're constantly coming up with new products.

For the new cook, an onslaught of so many ingredients can be overwhelming, but this cookbook was created to work with the limited time and new cooking skills of a college student. From snacks to feed a study group to sandwiches for a lunch on the run to a quick soup on a cold day, this book's got you covered. For dinner, you can use a microwave to whip up delicious dishes from your dorm room, tackle quick pasta recipes and hearty meals, and create special-occasion feasts for friends and family. There are even recipes for brain-boosting foods to help you out during exam weeks, and vegetarian options for when you need a little less meat. And, of course, what cookbook would be complete without a touch of dessert love? When you need a sweet treat in your life, tweak Trader Joe's products for a quick fix.

Chock-full of 150 recipes all using the best Trader Joe's has to offer, this book makes your job simple. Select a few recipes, head to your local Trader Joe's, and relish in the delicious creativity that comes from combining their ingredients to make a feast.

USING THIS BOOK

SUBSTITUTIONS

One of the greatest things about Trader Joe's is that in one shopping trip you can gather all the ingredients you'll need to make the recipes in this book. But sometimes you'll find that one location doesn't carry a certain item, that your absolute favorite Trader Joe's salsa has suddenly been discontinued, or that something you're craving is only stocked around the holidays. No worries— although the recipes here are all made using many TJ's specific ingredients, those can easily be substituted with a similar generic item. Or Trader Joe's often has a similar ingredient in stock: Can't find Trader Joe's Misto alla Griglia? See if they have Trader Joe's Grilled Eggplant and Zucchini Mélange. Use the recipes here as guidelines and you'll still be whipping up delicious dishes in no time and getting back to that term paper you've been putting off.

RECIPE ICONS

Whether you're looking for a quick snack to take to class or a heartier meal that you can still make with limited equipment (no stove? no problem!), handy icons accompany each recipe to quickly narrow your options: Microwave Only, One-Pot Cooking, Five-Minute Prep, No Cook, Grab and Go, and Vegetarian/Vegan. No matter what your cooking mood is, there's a recipe to match.

🔲	meals that can be prepared entirely in a microwave
🍲	meals that require just one pot
⏱	meals that can be prepared in five minutes or less
🚫	meals that require no cooking
🎒	meals that are great to take on the go
🌱	meals that are vegetarian or vegan

CHAPTER 1

SNACKS & NIBBLES

I f you've ever thought, "When will I need to make an appetizer?" then let me ask *you* a question in return: When is there a time an appetizer isn't appropriate? Think of it as food that's low on the commitment scale—fewer ingredients and minimal instructions all resulting in a smaller quantity of food. I could eat entire meals made straight from the nibbles in this chapter. In fact, I have.

So look at these recipes as a smorgasbord of sorts. When you want something to nibble on while walking to class, go for a recipe like the irresistible Bratwursts in a Blanket. Want to feed a study group coming to your dorm? Try Thai Red Curry Deviled Eggs or Mini Tostadas with Beef Brisket. Maybe you just want a plateful of Stuffed Mushrooms to feast on while cramming for an exam. Or serve up Spicy Boneless Chicken Pieces to cheer on a sports team. These recipes will make snack time much more rewarding than just tearing open the bag of chips you have lying around.

STUFFED MUSHROOMS

YIELD: 4 servings
PREP TIME: 10 minutes
COOKING TIME: 12 minutes

2 ounces cream cheese

¼ (6-ounce) bag baby spinach

2 tablespoons Trader Joe's
Roasted Red Pepper and
Artichoke Tapenade

8 ounces white mushrooms

Trader Joe's Grated Parmigiano-
Reggiano cheese (optional)

By removing the stem from a mushroom, you create a portable vessel to stuff with cheesy goodness.

1. Preheat the oven to 450°F. Spray a baking sheet with cooking spray.
2. Place the cream cheese and spinach in a microwave-safe bowl. Microwave on high until the cream cheese has softened, 30 seconds to 1 minute. Stir the spinach and cream cheese together, then stir in the tapenade until combined.
3. Remove the stems from the mushrooms and use a wet paper towel to wipe the outside of each mushroom clean. Spoon the mixture into each cavity and arrange the stuffed mushrooms on the prepared baking sheet.
4. Bake until the cheese is bubbly and the mushrooms are cooked, 10 to 12 minutes. Sprinkle with Parmigiano-Reggiano, if desired.

FRIED CHICKPEAS

YIELD: 4 servings
PREP TIME: 5 minutes
COOKING TIME: 10 minutes

¼ cup cornstarch

¼ cup flour

1 teaspoon kosher salt plus more for sprinkling

1 (15-ounce) can chickpeas, drained

canola oil, as needed

Whether you call them chickpeas or garbanzo beans, they're still delicious. The crispy fried coating gives way to the smooth softness of the beans in this vegan snack.

1. Line a plate with a paper towel. In a large bowl, combine the cornstarch, flour, and salt. Working in batches, add the chickpeas to the cornstarch mixture, coating thoroughly.
2. Toss the coated chickpeas into a strainer, shaking to remove excess coating.
3. In a large heavy deep pan, heat 1 inch of oil over high heat until shimmering.
4. When the oil is hot, add half the chickpeas and cook until crisp, 3 to 4 minutes. Transfer with a slotted spoon onto the prepared plate. Repeat with the remaining chickpeas. Sprinkle salt over the fried chickpeas.

OLIVE FOCACCIA

YIELD: 4 servings
PREP TIME: 10 minutes
COOKING TIME: 30 minutes

flour, as needed

1 ball Trader Joe's pizza dough,
at room temperature

1 tablespoon olive oil,
plus more as needed

3 tablespoons Trader Joe's Olive
Tapenade Spread, divided

2 Roma tomatoes,
thinly sliced lengthwise

½ teaspoon kosher salt

The great thing about tapenade is that all the work's been done for you and it can be used in many ways. Here, it's merged with pizza dough for an easy vegan focaccia.

1. Preheat the oven to 400°F.
2. Sprinkle 1 to 2 tablespoons flour onto a cutting board. Place the pizza dough on the cutting board and gently knead it. Then gently stretch the dough out with your fingers.
3. In an 8 x 12-inch glass baking dish, combine the oil and 1 tablespoon olive tapenade, and spread the mixture around the bottom of the dish.
4. Spread the pizza dough over the olive oil and tapenade, pressing the dough down into the bottom of the dish. Use your fingers to punch tiny indentations into the top of the dough.
5. Spread the remaining tapenade on top, then layer tomato slices over the top of the dough and sprinkle with the salt. Bake until the focaccia is puffy and golden, 25 to 30 minutes. Drizzle with olive oil and cut into pieces.

TABOULI-STUFFED MINI PITAS

YIELD: 8 to 10 mini pitas
PREP TIME: 10 minutes

Tabouli is a vegan Middle Eastern dish made with bulgur wheat, tomatoes, onions, and parsley tossed in olive oil and lemon juice.

⅓ (12-ounce) jar Trader Joe's Fire-Roasted Red and Yellow Peppers (about 2 peppers)

¾ cup Trader Joe's Tabouli Salad

3 tablespoons Trader Joe's Hummus with Freshly Ground Horseradish, or any other hummus

¼ teaspoon kosher salt

8 to 10 Trader Joe's Mini Pita Pockets

1. Chop the peppers into small dice.
2. In a small bowl, stir together the peppers, tabouli, hummus, and salt.
3. Slice a small opening in the top of each pita and stuff with the tabouli mixture.

GUACAMOLE WITH TOMATILLOS

YIELD: 4 servings
PREP TIME: 5 minutes

For this vegan guacamole, the avocado is paired with the tangy tomatillos in the salsa verde.

juice of ½ lime

1 scallion, chopped

2 tablespoons Trader Joe's Organic Tomatillo and Roasted Yellow Chili Sauce

½ jalapeño, seeds and ribs removed, minced (optional)

½ teaspoon kosher salt

2 avocados, diced (for tips on dicing, see page 152)

tortillas or chips

1. In a small bowl, whisk together the lime juice, scallion, tomatillo sauce, jalapeño, if using, and salt.
2. Add the avocado chunks and stir to combine.
3. Mash the avocado chunks with a fork until it's your preferred consistency. Serve with tortillas or chips.

BRATWURSTS IN A BLANKET

YIELD: 8 bratwursts in a blanket
PREP TIME: 10 minutes
COOKING TIME: 20 minutes

2 tablespoons Dijon mustard

1 tablespoon honey

1 (8-ounce) can Trader Joe's
Crescent Rolls

1 (7-ounce) package Trader
Joe's Fully-Cooked Bavarian
Bratwurst (8 sausages)

The slight tartness and full porkiness of the Trader Joe's Bavarian sausages make them fabulously addictive.

1. Preheat the oven to 375°F. Spray a baking sheet with cooking spray.
2. In a small bowl, combine the mustard and honey, stirring to thoroughly mix.
3. Unroll the crescent rolls from their can, placing them on a cutting board with the longest side of each crescent roll toward the bottom. Place a drop of the honey mustard on the bottom part of each crescent roll, followed by a bratwurst on top of the mustard. Set aside the remaining honey mustard.
4. Starting at the bottom of each roll, roll up the bratwurst in the crescent dough. Place the rolled bratwursts on the prepared baking sheet, making sure they are not touching each other.
5. Bake until the crescent rolls are golden brown, 18 to 20 minutes. Serve with the remaining honey mustard sauce.

JALAPEÑO CHEESE-STUFFED PEPPERS

YIELD: 24 stuffed pepper halves
PREP TIME: 10 minutes
COOKING TIME: 10 minutes

1 (1-pint) package Trader Joe's
Minisweet Peppers

½ cup Trader Joe's Pub Cheese
with Jalapeño

5 to 6 slices Trader Joe's Fully
Cooked Uncured Bacon

Trader Joe's pub cheese is made from cheddar, and it's all-natural yet silky and spreadable.

1. Preheat the oven to 425°F. Spray a baking sheet with cooking spray.
2. Cut each mini pepper lengthwise and use a spoon to remove the seeds. Using a spoon, fill the pepper halves with pub cheese, place them on the prepared baking sheet, and bake until the cheese has melted, 5 to 8 minutes.
3. Meanwhile, arrange the bacon slices between layers of paper towels in a small microwave-safe dish. Microwave on high until crispy, 30 to 45 seconds. Crumble the bacon into bits.
4. Sprinkle the bacon over the cheesy peppers.

THAI RED CURRY DEVILED EGGS

YIELD: 12 deviled eggs
PREP TIME: 10 minutes

1 (9.3-ounce) package Trader
Joe's Cage Free Fresh Hard-
Cooked Peeled Eggs (6 eggs)

2 tablespoons mayonnaise

2 tablespoons Trader Joe's Thai
Red Curry Sauce

1 teaspoon lime juice

1 scallion, chopped, plus extra
for garnish

¼ teaspoon kosher salt

The secret ingredient in these babies is Trader Joe's Thai Red Curry Sauce, which adds an exotic flare.

1. Cut each hard-cooked egg in half lengthwise. Scoop the yolks out into a small bowl.
2. Add the mayonnaise, curry sauce, lime juice, scallion, and salt to the bowl with the yolks. Mash the ingredients together until combined.
3. Spoon the yolk mixture into the egg white halves and garnish with a few pieces of scallion.

Note: If TJ's hard-cooked eggs are not available, see page 153.

SPICY BONELESS CHICKEN PIECES

YIELD: 4 servings
PREP TIME: 10 minutes
COOKING TIME: 15 minutes

¼ cup canola oil

1 (22-ounce) package Trader Joe's Mandarin Orange Chicken

½ cup Trader Joe's Jalapeño Pepper Hot Sauce

4 tablespoons unsalted butter

¼ cup honey

Coating Trader Joe's Mandarin Orange Chicken in a mixture of hot sauce and butter creates boneless buffalo wings in a snap.

1. Line a plate with a paper towel. Heat the oil in a large skillet over medium-high heat until shimmering.
2. Discard the orange sauce from the chicken. Add the chicken pieces to the skillet and cook until crispy, 8 to 10 minutes, turning them over halfway through. Transfer the chicken to the prepared plate.
3. In a microwave-safe dish, place the hot sauce, butter, and honey. Microwave on high until the butter is melted and the sauce is warm, about 1 minute. Pour the hot sauce mixture into a large bowl along with the chicken pieces. Coat the chicken pieces with the hot sauce.

SLOPPY JOE NACHOS

YIELD: 4 servings
PREP TIME: 5 minutes
COOKING TIME: 10 minutes

1 (12-ounce) package frozen Trader Joe's Turkey Bolognese

1½ tablespoons brown sugar

1 tablespoon vinegar

1 tablespoon ketchup

½ (11.5-ounce) jar Trader Joe's Queso Cheese Dip

½ (16-ounce) bag Trader Joe's Organic Yellow Corn Tortilla Chip Rounds

This playful spin on nachos is Super Bowl food at its best.

1. Microwave the turkey Bolognese according to the package directions.
2. Carefully remove the Bolognese from the microwave. Add the brown sugar, vinegar, and ketchup to the carton, stirring to combine.
3. Pour the queso dip into a microwave-safe dish and microwave on high until warm, 2 to 3 minutes.
4. Layer a plate with the tortilla chips and pour the warm Bolognese mixture over top. Drizzle queso dip over the chips.

PINWHEELS *with* SPINACH *and* PROSCIUTTO

YIELD: about 20 pinwheels
PREP TIME: 10 minutes
COOKING TIME: 15 minutes

1 tablespoon flour

1 (8-ounce) can Trader Joe's Crescent Rolls

1 (4-ounce) package Trader Joe's Traditional Prosciutto

½ cup Trader Joe's Spinach and Sour Cream Dip

Italian for "ham," prosciutto is ham that has been seasoned, salt cured, air dried, and pressed.

1. Preheat the oven to 400°F. Spray a baking sheet with cooking spray.

2. Dust a cutting board with the flour. Transfer the crescent dough in one piece from the tube onto the cutting board. Roll the dough out into a rectangle and pinch the creases together.

3. Layer the dough with 3 pieces of prosciutto, spread the spinach dip in an even layer on top of the prosciutto, then layer 3 more pieces of prosciutto on top.

4. Roll the dough up into a log, starting with the long side of the rectangle. Cut the log into rounds about ¾ inch thick. Arrange the pinwheels on the prepared baking sheet so they aren't touching each other.

5. Bake until the dough is golden brown, about 15 minutes.

PORK BUNS *with* BROCCOLI SLAW

YIELD: 4 pork buns
PREP TIME: 5 minutes
COOKING TIME: 5 minutes

1½ cups Trader Joe's Organic
Broccoli Slaw

⅓ cup mayonnaise

1 teaspoon Trader Joe's Jalapeño
Pepper Hot Sauce (optional)

1 teaspoon soy sauce

2 teaspoons white vinegar

1 (8-ounce) package frozen
Trader Ming's Chinese Style
Pork Buns

Barbecued pork and coleslaw are a tasty combo that gets an Asian spin in this recipe.

1. Stir together slaw, mayonnaise, hot sauce, if using, soy sauce, and vinegar in a medium bowl.
2. Place the pork buns on a microwave-safe dish and cover with a damp paper towel. Microwave on high until warm, about 45 seconds.
3. Carefully cut off the top one-third of each pork bun, discarding the extra dough. Pile slaw onto the pork buns and serve open-faced.

FRITO PIE

YIELD: 4 servings
PREP TIME: 10 minutes
COOKING TIME: 5 minutes

½ (4-ounce) can Trader Joe's
New Mexico Hatch Valley Fire
Roasted Diced Green Chiles

½ cup sour cream

salt

½ (15-ounce) can Trader Joe's
Beef Chili with Beans

½ (14½-ounce) bag Trader Joe's
Organic Corn Chip Dippers

1 cup Trader Joe's Shredded
Cheddar Cheese

Frito Pie is a Texan dish that pairs corn chips with chili and cheese. This is prime football-watching food.

1. In a small bowl, combine the green chiles and sour cream. Add salt to taste and stir.
2. Microwave the chili on high until warm, 2 to 3 minutes.
3. On a large plate, spread the chips in a single layer. Pour the chili on top of the chips and sprinkle with the cheese. Garnish with dollops of the green chile sour cream.

MINI TOSTADAS *with* BEEF BRISKET

YIELD: 4 servings
PREP TIME: 10 minutes
COOKING TIME: 5 minutes

Tortilla chips are layered with brisket and melted pimento cheese for heavenly mini tostadas.

1 (16-ounce) package Trader Joe's Pulled Beef Brisket in Smoky BBQ Sauce

½ (16-ounce) bag Trader Joe's Organic Blue Corn Tortilla Chips

1 cup Trader Joe's Pimento Cheese Spread

1. Preheat the oven to 400°F. Line a rimmed baking sheet with foil.
2. Microwave the beef brisket according to the package directions.
3. On the prepared baking sheet, spread a layer of tortilla chips. Using a fork, add a little beef brisket to each chip, followed by a layer of pimento cheese.
4. Bake until the cheese has melted, about 5 minutes.

SWEET CHILI WINGS

YIELD: 12 wings
PREP TIME: 5 minutes
COOKING TIME: 30 minutes

Trader Joe's has many sauces to inspire your wings, and I enjoy the sweet and spicy flavor of the Sweet Chili Sauce.

12 Trader Joe's Organic Free Range Split Chicken Wings

1 teaspoon baking soda

1 teaspoon kosher salt

¾ cup Trader Joe's Sweet Chili Sauce

¼ cup cold unsalted butter, cut into pieces

1 tablespoon Trader Joe's Jalapeño Pepper Hot Sauce (optional)

1. Preheat the oven to 425°F. Line a rimmed baking sheet with foil.
2. Place the wings on the prepared baking sheet, sprinkle with the baking soda and salt, and toss to coat the wings. Spread the wings in a single layer, and bake until the wings are crispy and the meat is fully cooked, 20 to 25 minutes.
3. Combine the chili sauce, butter, and hot sauce, if using, in a microwave-safe dish. Microwave on high until the butter is melted and the sauce is warm, about 1 minute. Stir.
4. Transfer the wings to a large bowl and add the sauce. Using a large spoon or tongs, toss the cooked wings with the sauce to coat.

Note: The baking soda makes for a crispier hot wing.

CHAPTER 2

SANDWICHES & SALADS

Sandwiches and salads are the go-to lunch option for many people, but it's easy to get stuck in a rut. Before you know it, you're eating the same ham and cheese every day of the week. That's an avoidable problem—think of sandwiches and salads as empty canvasses on which you can put pretty much anything. Just about any meat, cheese, vegetable, and sauce can be put on a sandwich. And the options for salads are just as vast. Trader Joe's makes it easy with options like pulled pork that's been smoked for hours or eggs that are already hard-cooked. Your only job is to put it all together.

And don't feel like you can make only these recipes to pack for lunch. French Toast and Sausage Sandwiches are perfect to munch on while trekking to class in the morning, and a Muffuletta Sandwich or Barbecue Salad with Ranch Dressing is hearty enough to satisfy dinnertime hunger.

GRILLED FOUR-CHEESE SANDWICHES

YIELD: 2 sandwiches
PREP TIME: 5 minutes
COOKING TIME: 5 to 8 minutes

4 slices Trader Joe's Texas Toast

yellow mustard, as needed

1 cup Trader Joe's Shredded Smoked Cheese Blend

2 tablespoons unsalted butter, divided

Shredded cheese makes for easier melting, and the thick Texas Toast is the bread of choice, but any bread will do in a pinch.

1. Spread 2 slices of Texas toast with mustard. Mound with the shredded cheese and top with another slice of Texas toast.
2. In a nonstick pan, melt 1 tablespoon butter over medium-high heat. Add both sandwiches to the pan and flatten them with a spatula.
3. Cook until the bottom sides are golden, 1 to 2 minutes.
4. Add the remaining 1 tablespoon butter to the pan, flipping the sandwiches over. Cook until the second side is golden, 1 to 2 minutes.

ALMOND BUTTER *and* BANANA SANDWICHES

YIELD: 2 sandwiches
PREP TIME: 5 minutes

4 slices Trader Joe's Soft 10 Grain Bread, or another type of bread, toasted if desired

Trader Joe's Creamy Almond Butter with Sea Salt, as needed

2 teaspoons honey

1 banana, sliced

This is an absolute staple for my breakfast, and I usually make it open-faced. It's easy, healthy, and delicious.

1. Spread 2 slices of bread with almond butter and drizzle with honey.
2. Divide the banana pieces between the slices of bread, and top each one with a second slice.

Note: Leftover Almond Butter and Banana Sandwich? No problem, see page 154.

FRENCH TOAST *and* SAUSAGE SANDWICHES

YIELD: 3 sandwiches
PREP TIME: 5 minutes
COOKING TIME: 5 minutes

1 (8-ounce) box Trader Joe's
Veggie Sausage Patties

1 (12-ounce) box Trader Joe's
Low Fat French Toast

2 tablespoons unsalted butter,
cut into pieces

2 tablespoons maple syrup

This quick and easy sandwich is super simple and deliriously delicious.

1. Microwave the sausage patties according to the package directions and cook the French toast in the toaster until golden.
2. In a small bowl, microwave the butter on high until just softened, 5 to 10 seconds. Stir in the maple syrup.
3. Lay half of the toast slices on a cutting board and soak with the maple syrup and butter.
4. Slice the patties in half and place 2 on each of the toast slices. Top with the remaining toast.

GRILLED CHICKEN STRIPS on NAAN with RED PEPPER SPREAD

YIELD: 2 sandwiches
PREP TIME: 10 minutes
COOKING TIME: 2 minutes

2 pieces Trader Joe's Masala Tandoori Naan

2 tablespoons Trader Joe's Red Pepper Spread with Eggplant and Garlic

½ (12-ounce) package Trader Joe's Grilled Chicken Strips

4 slices Swiss cheese

Trader Joe's Red Pepper Spread with Eggplant and Garlic adds a massive spark of flavor to enhance the sandwich.

1. Arrange the naan in a microwave-safe dish. Spread 1 tablespoon red pepper spread on top of each piece of naan. Layer with the chicken strips and top with the cheese.
2. Microwave on high until the cheese is melted, about 1 minute.

MUFFULETTA SANDWICHES

YIELD: 2 sandwiches
PREP TIME: 10 minutes

2 pieces Trader Giotto's Focaccini, or other crusty rolls

yellow mustard, as needed

1½ tablespoons Trader Joe's Green Olive Tapenade

4 slices turkey bologna

½ (7-ounce) package Trader Joe's Smoked Turkey Breast

2 slices Swiss cheese

2 Roma tomatoes, sliced

A New Orleans specialty, the muffuletta sandwich is a crusty roll filled with meat like ham and salami and topped with a mixture of chopped olives.

1. Slice each focaccini in half. Spread the bottom layer of each focaccini with mustard and the top with tapenade. On the bottom half of each sandwich, layer the bologna, turkey, cheese, and tomato.
2. Cover with the top layers and cut each sandwich in half.

TUNA SALAD SANDWICHES

YIELD: 2 sandwiches
PREP TIME: 5 minutes

It's the addition of a little lemon juice along with the sweetness of the relish that makes this tuna salad recipe shine.

3½ tablespoons mayonnaise, divided

1 teaspoon lemon juice

½ teaspoon salt

¼ teaspoon ground pepper

2 tablespoons Trader Joe's Organic Sweet Pickle Relish

2 (5-ounce) cans Trader Joe's Albacore Solid White Tuna in Water, drained

4 slices Trader Joe's Texas Toast, or any other sandwich bread

1. In a small bowl, combine 2½ tablespoons mayonnaise and the lemon juice, salt, pepper, and relish, and stir to combine.
2. Mix in the tuna with a fork until combined. Taste and adjust the seasoning as needed. Spread the remaining 1 tablespoon mayonnaise among all 4 slices of bread. Divide the tuna salad between 2 slices of bread, then top the salad with the remaining slices.

FRIED FISH SANDWICHES

YIELD: 2 sandwiches
PREP TIME: 10 minutes
COOKING TIME: 25 minutes

Trader Joe's Panko Breaded Tilapia Fillet is fried fish at its best without all of the labor-intensive work.

1 fillet frozen Trader Joe's Panko Breaded Tilapia Fillets

2 tablespoons mayonnaise

2 teaspoons Trader Joe's Organic Sweet Pickle Relish

1 teaspoon lemon juice

2 Trader Joe's Honey Wheat Hamburger Buns

1. Preheat the oven to 425°F. Line a rimmed baking sheet with foil.
2. Place the fish fillet on the prepared baking sheet and bake until hot, 20 to 25 minutes. Meanwhile, in a small bowl, make a tartar sauce by stirring together the mayonnaise, relish, and lemon juice.
3. Carefully remove the fish from the oven and split the fillet in half horizontally with a knife. Layer the bottom halves of the buns with the tartar sauce and fish. Add the bun tops.

BUFFALO CHICKEN WRAPS *with* BLUE CHEESE *and* CARROTS

YIELD: 2 wraps
PREP TIME: 10 minutes
COOKING TIME: 5 to 7 minutes

12 to 14 frozen Trader Joe's Buffalo Chicken Wings Fully Cooked

2 Trader Joe's Habanero Lime Flour Tortillas, or other tortillas

2 teaspoons Trader Joe's Blue Cheese Roasted Pecan Dip

½ (10-ounce) bag shredded carrots

This sandwich isn't for those wary of spice. Between the fiery buffalo chicken wings and the zesty habanero tortillas, this wrap packs a lot of heat.

1. Microwave the wings according to the package directions. When the wings are cool enough to handle, remove the meat from the bones. Discard the bones.
2. Lay the tortillas on a cutting board. Spread 1 teaspoon blue cheese dip in a line down the middle of each tortilla.
3. Layer the chicken and carrots on top of the blue cheese dip on the tortillas. Roll the wraps burrito-style, tucking the bottom up before rolling sideways.

EGG SALAD SANDWICHES

YIELD: 2 sandwiches
PREP TIME: 5 minutes
COOKING TIME: 5 minutes

1 (9.3-ounce) package Trader Joe's Cage Free Fresh Hard-Cooked Peeled Eggs (6 eggs)

3 tablespoons mayonnaise, divided

¼ teaspoon salt

¼ teaspoon freshly ground black pepper

1 celery rib, chopped

4 slices Trader Joe's Soft 10 Grain Bread, or another type of bread, toasted if desired

Celery adds a slight crunch to contrast with the silkiness of the egg salad. For extra oomph, add ham or even prosciutto.

1. In a small bowl, mash the hard-cooked eggs with a fork. Add 2 tablespoons mayonnaise and the salt, pepper, and celery, and stir to combine. Taste and adjust the seasonings as needed.
2. Spread the bread slices with the remaining 1 tablespoon mayonnaise. Mound the egg salad onto 2 slices of bread, then top with the remaining slices.

Note: If TJ's hard-cooked eggs are not available, see page 153.

PULLED PORK SANDWICHES

YIELD: 4 sandwiches
PREP TIME: 10 minutes
COOKING TIME: 5 minutes

½ (16-ounce) package Trader Joe's Pulled Pork in Smoky Barbecue Sauce

½ (10-ounce) bag shredded green cabbage

1 tablespoon mayonnaise

2 tablespoons chopped Trader Joe's Organic Sweet Bread and Butter Pickles, plus 1½ tablespoons pickle juice

kosher salt and freshly ground black pepper

4 Trader Joe's Michette Rolls, or other rolls

Trader Joe's smoked pulled pork lets you enjoy all the delicious smokiness of the meat without the effort of having to make it yourself.

1. Microwave the pulled pork according to the package directions.
2. In a small bowl, make the cole slaw by stirring together the cabbage, mayonnaise, chopped pickles, and pickle juice. Season to taste with salt and pepper.
3. Spread pulled pork on the bottom half of each roll. Add the coleslaw and the top halves of the rolls.

BLT SANDWICHES

YIELD: 2 sandwiches
PREP TIME: 5 minutes
COOKING TIME: 5 minutes

8 slices Trader Joe's Fully Cooked Uncured Bacon

4 slices Trader Joe's Soft 10 Grain Bread, toasted

½ cup Trader Joe's Julienne Sliced Sun Dried Tomatoes in Olive Oil, drained

¼ cup mayonnaise

kosher salt and freshly ground black pepper

¼ cup lettuce leaves, like Trader Joe's Very American Salad

Does it get any better than a sandwich stuffed with crisp bacon, tomatoes, and crunchy lettuce?

1. Arrange the bacon slices between layers of paper towels in a microwave-safe dish. Microwave on high power until crispy, 30 seconds to 1 minute.
2. In a small bowl, stir together the sun dried tomatoes and mayonnaise to combine. Season to taste with salt and pepper, and stir again.
3. Spread tomato mayonnaise onto 2 bread slices. Layer with bacon slices and lettuce leaves. Top with the remaining 2 slices of bread.

CHILEAN-STYLE HOT DOGS

YIELD: 4 hot dogs
PREP TIME: 5 minutes
COOKING TIME: 5 minutes

4 Trader Joe's Honey Wheat Hot Dog Buns

4 Trader Joe's All Natural Uncured All-Beef Hot Dogs

mayonnaise, as needed

2 Roma tomatoes, sliced

1 avocado, sliced
(for slicing tips, see page 152)

A friend from South America introduced me to Chilean-style hot dogs—hot dogs layered on hard buns with mayonnaise and slices of tomato and avocado.

1. Preheat the oven to 400°F. Arrange the hot dog buns on a baking sheet and place in the oven until toasted, just 1 to 2 minutes.
2. Meanwhile, wrap the hot dogs in a damp paper towel, and microwave on high until hot, about 1 minute.
3. Carefully remove the toasted buns from the oven. Spread each bun with mayonnaise and add the hot dogs. Garnish each one with tomato and avocado slices.

MEATBALL SUB

YIELD: 2 servings
PREP TIME: 10 minutes
COOKING TIME: 10 minutes

½ (16-ounce) package frozen
Trader Giotto's Meatballs Fully
Cooked (about 6 meatballs)

½ cup Trader Giotto's Organic
Tomato Basil Marinara

1 (12-ounce) package Trader
Giotto's Garlic Bread Sticks

2 slices provolone cheese, halved

Trader Giotto's Garlic Bread Sticks are a great start to building a meatball sub.

1. Preheat the oven to 400°F. Line a rimmed baking sheet with foil.
2. Cut each meatball in half and place in a microwave-safe dish. Microwave on high until slightly warm, about 1 minute. Pour the marinara sauce over the meatballs and microwave on high until the sauce is warm, about 1 minute.
3. Split 2 of the bread sticks in half lengthwise, cutting only three-quarters of the way through to keep the halves attached. Place the bread on the prepared baking sheet, split-side up. Evenly divide the heated meatballs and marinara sauce between the split bread sticks and top each one with 2 cheese halves.
4. Bake the sandwiches until the cheese is melted and the bread is toasted, 7 to 10 minutes.

TROPICAL FRUIT SALAD

YIELD: 2 servings
PREP TIME: 10 minutes

1 (16-ounce) container Trader Joe's Tropical Fruit Medley

2 teaspoons honey

juice of ½ lemon

1 apple, cut into bite-size pieces

1 pear, cut into bite-size pieces

Trader Joe's Tropical Fruit Medley, which includes mango, pineapple, and papaya, serves as a starting point for the makings of a tasty fruit salad.

1. Drain the tropical fruit, reserving the juices, and cut the fruit into bite-size pieces.

2. In a medium bowl, stir together the fruit juice, honey, and lemon juice. Add the chopped tropical fruit, apple, and pear, and stir.

CAESAR SALAD 2.0

YIELD: 2 servings
PREP TIME: 5 minutes

1 (15-ounce) bag Trader Joe's Caesar Salad with Croutons, Shredded Parmesan Cheese and Dressing

½ cup Trader Joe's Julienne Sliced Sun Dried Tomatoes in Olive Oil, drained

½ cup pitted kalamata olives

½ (12-ounce) package Trader Joe's Grilled Lemon Pepper Chicken

By taking Trader Joe's Caesar Salad and elevating it with a few Mediterranean ingredients, this dish has the makings of a meal.

1. In a medium bowl, place the lettuce from the salad mix. Top the lettuce with the sun dried tomatoes, olives, and chicken. Toss to combine.
2. Add the cheese from the salad mix and drizzle with the dressing. Toss gently to combine.

BARBECUE SALAD *with* RANCH DRESSING

YIELD: 2 servings
PREP TIME: 10 minutes
COOKING TIME: 5 minutes

½ (16-ounce) package Trader Joe's Pulled Chicken Breast in Smoky Barbecue Sauce

½ (16-ounce) bag Trader Joe's Very American Salad

2 Roma tomatoes, diced

1 cucumber, diced

½ cup Trader Joe's Shredded Smoked Cheese Blend

Trader Joe's Lowfat Parmesan Ranch Dressing, as needed

A blend of iceberg lettuce, romaine lettuce, and cabbage is perfect for a barbecue salad.

1. Microwave the chicken according to the package directions.
2. In a medium bowl, place the salad, tomatoes, cucumbers, and cheese. Drizzle with the ranch dressing and toss to combine.
3. Transfer the salad to plates and top with the chicken.

CHICKEN SALAD-STUFFED TOMATOES

YIELD: 2 servings
PREP TIME: 10 minutes

½ (12-ounce) container
Trader Joe's Wine Country
Chicken Salad with Cranberries
and Pecans

½ Granny Smith apple,
cut into bite-size pieces

½ cup chopped celery

kosher salt and freshly ground
black pepper

4 Roma tomatoes

The apple adds a tartness to this sweet chicken salad and the celery brings a nice crunch, mandatory for any salad, in my book.

1. In a small bowl, stir together the chicken salad, apple, and celery. Season to taste with salt and pepper.
2. Cut the top ¼ inch off each tomato. Hollow out each tomato and fill with chicken salad.

ANTIPASTO SALAD

YIELD: 2 servings
PREP TIME: 10 minutes

½ (8-ounce) package
sopressata salami

1 (14-ounce) can artichoke
hearts, drained

1 (8-ounce) jar Trader Joe's
Dolmas

1 (12-ounce) jar Trader Joe's
Giant White Beans

kosher salt and freshly ground
black pepper

The word antipasto *refers to the traditional first course of an Italian meal, which includes a platter of cured meats, artichokes, olives, and cheeses.*

1. Cube the salami into bite-size pieces. Place in a medium bowl.
2. Cut the artichoke hearts and the dolmas in half. Add to the bowl with the salami. Add the entire jar of beans to the bowl, stirring to combine. Season to taste with salt and pepper.

GREEK PASTA SALAD

YIELD: 4 servings
PREP TIME: 10 minutes
COOKING TIME: 5 minutes

½ teaspoon kosher salt, plus more for boiling the pasta

2 (10-ounce) packages Trader Joe's Perline Pasta and Prosciutto

juice of 1 lemon

⅓ cup olive oil

½ teaspoon dried oregano or dried thyme (optional)

¼ teaspoon freshly ground black pepper

1 pint grape tomatoes

1 cucumber, peeled and chopped into bite-size pieces

1½ cups Trader Joe's Marinated Artichokes, cut into bite-size pieces

⅓ cup Trader Joe's Feta Cheese with Mediterranean Herbs

This pasta salad can be eaten warm, cold, or at room temperature. It's easy to whip up and will please a crowd without costing a ton of cash.

1. Bring a medium pot of salted water to a boil over high heat. Cook the perline pasta until al dente (see page 153), 2 to 3 minutes. Drain the pasta in a colander.

2. Meanwhile, in a large bowl, whisk together the lemon juice, olive oil, oregano, salt, and pepper.

3. Add the pasta to the bowl with the dressing, along with the tomatoes, cucumber, and artichoke hearts. Stir with a large spoon. Taste and adjust the seasonings with salt and pepper, as needed. Top with the cheese.

SOUPS

To break it down plain and simple, soup just makes me happy. In my world, there's nothing more comforting than slurping a bowl of homemade soup. Most complaints about making soup are about it being too time-consuming. Not so with these recipes, thanks to Trader Joe's easy ingredients. And words cannot even describe my love for Trader Joe's Savory Chicken Concentrate. It takes

up so little room in the cabinet compared to its equivalent of chicken broth cans. As long as you're stocked with these little packets, homemade soup in minutes is within reach.

It's worth noting that for an avid soup maker, an immersion blender is an inexpensive, worthwhile investment: It's compact and allows you to purée soups right in the pot.

MISO SOUP *with* TOFU *and* SPINACH

YIELD: 2 servings
PREP TIME: 5 minutes
COOKING TIME: 10 minutes

Adding spinach and tofu to Trader Joe's Instant Miso Soup really bulks it up into a heartier vegan meal.

3 cups water

2 (.94-ounce) packets Trader Joe's Instant Miso Soup

½ (6-ounce) bag baby spinach

½ (14-ounce) package Trader Joe San Firm Organic Tofu, cut into bite-size pieces

2 scallions, chopped, for garnish

1. In a small pot, bring the water to a boil over high heat. Whisk in the soup mix. Add the spinach, stirring until wilted, about 1 minute, then add the tofu pieces and stir.
2. Remove the soup from heat and ladle it into bowls. Garnish with the scallions.

PESTO TORTELLINI SOUP

YIELD: 2 servings
PREP TIME: 10 minutes
COOKING TIME: 15 minutes

Turn the Trader Joe's Pesto Tortellini Bowl into a pesto-filled basil soup with the bite of arugula and melted Parmesan shavings.

1 (9.5-ounce) container Trader Joe's Pesto Tortellini Bowl

2 cups chicken broth, or 2 cups hot water plus 2 (9.6-gram) pouches Trader Joe's Savory Chicken Concentrate

2 tablespoons Trader Giotto's Pesto alla Genovese, or more

½ teaspoon kosher salt, or more

¼ teaspoon ground black pepper, or more

½ (7-ounce) bag arugula

¼ cup Trader Joe's Shaved Grana Padano Parmesan

1. Microwave the tortellini according to the package directions.
2. Meanwhile, add the chicken broth, pesto, salt, and pepper to a medium pot and bring it to a boil over high heat. Reduce the heat to low and simmer. Add the contents of the tortellini bowl to the simmering broth. Add the arugula and stir until wilted.
3. Taste and adjust the seasoning with salt and pepper, or add more pesto, as needed. Top with Parmesan.

Note: Leftover pesto? No problem, see page 154.

THAI CARROT SOUP

YIELD: 2 servings
PREP TIME: 5 minutes
COOKING TIME: 25 minutes

1 (10-ounce) bag shredded carrots

1 (14-ounce) can light coconut milk

1 cup vegetable broth, or 1 cup hot water plus 1 (9.6-gram) pouch Trader Joe's Vegetable Concentrate

½ cup Trader Joe's Thai Yellow Curry Sauce

kosher salt and freshly ground black pepper

This dairy-free soup is a blend of flavors that tastes like it takes much longer to prepare than it does.

1. Coarsely chop the shredded carrots into bite-size pieces.
2. Add the carrots, coconut milk, vegetable broth, and curry sauce to a medium pot and bring to a boil over high heat. Once the soup is boiling, reduce the heat to medium and simmer until the carrots are fully cooked, 15 to 20 minutes.
3. Season to taste with salt and pepper.

RICE *and* BEANS SOUP

YIELD: 4 servings
PREP TIME: 5 minutes
COOKING TIME: 15 minutes

1 (32-ounce) box Trader Joe's Latin-Style Black Bean Soup

½ (16-ounce) bag frozen Trader Joe's Roasted Corn

1 cup Trader José's Habanero and Lime Salsa

¾ teaspoon kosher salt

½ teaspoon freshly ground black pepper

1 (10.5-ounce) package Trader Joe's Brown Rice Fully Cooked

It's the comfort of rice and beans transformed into vegan soup. Eat this soup immediately after preparing it, otherwise the rice soaks up the liquid.

1. In a medium pot, add the soup, corn, salsa, salt, and pepper, and bring to a boil over high heat.
2. Reduce the heat to low and simmer for 10 minutes to allow the flavors to mingle.
3. Add the brown rice, stirring to combine. Simmer just a few more minutes.

DOUBLE BUTTERNUT SQUASH SOUP *with* GORGONZOLA RAVIOLI

YIELD: 2 servings
PREP TIME: 8 minutes
COOKING TIME: 15 minutes

1 (12-ounce) bag Trader Joe's Cut Butternut Squash

½ (32-ounce) box Trader Joe's Organic Low Sodium Butternut Squash Soup

½ cup water

½ teaspoon kosher salt

½ teaspoon freshly ground black pepper

1 (9-ounce) package Trader Giotto's Gorgonzola Cheese Ravioli

2 cubes frozen parsley (optional)

With both a butternut squash soup base and squash, this soup's sweetness is balanced nicely with the salty bite from the gorgonzola ravioli.

1. Microwave the butternut squash according to the package directions. Carefully transfer it from the plastic package to a cutting board. Let cool for a couple of minutes, then chop the squash into bite-size pieces.

2. Add the butternut squash soup, water, salt, and pepper to a medium pot and bring to a boil over high heat. Add the ravioli, making sure that all the ravioli pieces are submerged in the liquid. Reduce the heat to medium and cook until the ravioli are tender, 8 to 10 minutes.

3. Remove the soup from the heat and carefully cut each ravioli into quarters. Garnish with the parsley, if desired.

CURRIED LENTIL SOUP

YIELD: 2 servings
PREP TIME: 5 minutes
COOKING TIME: 15 minutes

½ tablespoon canola oil

½ (14.5-ounce) container Trader Joe's Mirepoix

2 cups vegetable broth, or 2 cups hot water plus 2 (9.6-gram) pouches Trader Joe's Vegetable Concentrate

1 (8-ounce) package Trader Joe's Black Beluga Lentils

¼ cup Trader Joe's Thai Red Curry Sauce

1 tablespoon curry powder

juice of ½ lemon

kosher salt and freshly ground black pepper

Lentils can take a little time to cook, but not so with the already prepared beluga lentils from Trader Joe's.

1. In a medium pot, heat the oil over medium heat until shimmering. Add the mirepoix and sauté until the vegetables are slightly softened, about 5 minutes.
2. Add the vegetable broth, lentils, curry sauce, curry powder, and lemon juice, stirring to combine. Let the soup simmer over medium heat for about 10 minutes.
3. Season to taste with salt and pepper.

Note: Mirepoix is a mixture of chopped carrots, celery, and onions that's a base for many soup, stew, and sauce recipes. Trader Joe's makes it easy by doing all the chopping for you.

SEAFOOD STEW *with* GARLIC BREAD CROUTONS

YIELD: 2 servings
PREP TIME: 10 minutes
COOKING TIME: 25 minutes

½ (16-ounce) package Trader Joe's Seafood Sausage (2 sausages)

1 tablespoon canola oil, divided

1 (9-ounce) box frozen Trader Joe's Garlic Bread

1 teaspoon Trader Joe's Crushed Garlic

1 (14.5-ounce) can Trader Joe's Organic Tomato Bisque

¾ cup water

½ teaspoon kosher salt

¼ teaspoon freshly ground black pepper

1 (1-pound) package Trader Joe's Steamer Clams in Garlic Butter Sauce

This luxurious stew is a cinch to put together. The clams already have a butter sauce that adds a delightful seafood taste.

1. Preheat the oven to 425°F.
2. Cut a slit into each seafood sausage. Peel away the casings from the sausages and crumble the seafood into pieces. Over medium-high heat in a medium pot, heat ½ tablespoon oil until shimmering. Add the seafood sausage pieces and sauté just briefly until cooked, 2 to 3 minutes, stirring constantly. Remove from the heat and transfer the sausage pieces to a plate.
3. Place the garlic bread on a baking sheet and bake until golden and toasted, 10 to 12 minutes.
4. Meanwhile, heat the remaining ½ tablespoon oil in the medium pot over medium-high heat. Add the garlic and cook, stirring constantly, until golden, about 30 seconds. Stir in the tomato bisque soup, water, salt, and pepper. Bring the soup to a boil, then reduce the heat to low and simmer.
5. Meanwhile, prepare the clams according to the package directions, then let them sit for 2 minutes.
6. Cut the garlic bread into bite-size pieces for croutons.
7. Add the reserved seafood sausage pieces and clams with butter sauce to the soup. Stir, and cook just 1 minute. Remove from the heat and top with the croutons.

MEXICAN TORTILLA SOUP *with* AVOCADO *and* TORTILLA CHIPS

YIELD: 2 servings
PREP TIME: 15 minutes
COOKING TIME: 20 minutes

2 cups chicken broth, or 2 cups hot water plus 2 (9.6-gram) pouches Trader Joe's Savory Chicken Concentrate

½ (28-ounce) can Trader Joe's Diced Organic Tomatoes in Tomato Juice

2 tablespoons Trader Joe's Taco Seasoning Mix, or more

½ teaspoon kosher salt, or more

¼ teaspoon freshly ground black pepper, or more

2 cups chicken meat from Trader Joe's Fully Cooked Seasoned Rotisserie-Style Roasted Chicken

juice of 1 lime

1 ounce cilantro, leaves plucked from stems

1 avocado, diced (for dicing tips, see page 152)

¼ (16-ounce) bag Trader Joe's Salsa Tortilla Chips, crumbled

The chicken and tomato base is enhanced by the richness of avocado, the crunch of tortilla chips, and the flavors of Mexican seasonings.

1. In a medium pot, add the chicken broth, tomatoes, taco seasoning, salt, and pepper, and stir to combine. Bring to a boil over high heat. Reduce the heat to medium-low. Add the chicken pieces and lime juice and simmer for 10 minutes.
2. Adjust the seasoning with salt, pepper, or taco seasoning, as needed. Garnish with cilantro, avocado, and crumbled chips.

CHICKEN *and* DUMPLINGS

YIELD: 2 servings
PREP TIME: 10 minutes
COOKING TIME: 20 minutes

4 cups chicken broth, or 4 cups hot water plus 4 (9.6-gram) pouches Trader Joe's Savory Chicken Concentrate

½ (16-ounce) can Trader Joe's Buttermilk Biscuits (4 biscuits)

1 (16-ounce) package Trader Joe's Just Chicken white meat

½ teaspoon kosher salt

¼ teaspoon freshly ground black pepper

2 tablespoons chopped chives (optional)

Chicken and dumplings usually takes a lot of work. The shortcut here is the buttermilk biscuits, which simmer in the chicken broth to create airy, fluffy dumplings.

1. In a medium pot, bring the chicken broth to a boil over high heat.
2. Meanwhile, remove 4 biscuits from the package, and cut each biscuit into three rows horizontally and vertically, creating 9 pieces from each biscuit.
3. When the chicken broth begins boiling, carefully drop in each biscuit piece.
4. Reduce the heat to medium and cover the pot. Cook until the biscuit pieces are fully cooked and soft, about 15 minutes. Use a slotted spoon to remove 1 dumpling; cut it in half and taste to check for doneness.
5. Stir in the chicken pieces, salt, and pepper. Cook until the chicken is hot throughout, 2 or 3 minutes, and garnish with chives, if using.

Note: The biscuits must be dropped into the liquid individually or they'll stick together.

ANDOUILLE *and* CHICKPEA SOUP

YIELD: 2 servings
PREP TIME: 10 minutes
COOKING TIME: 25 minutes

½ (12.8-ounce) package Trader Joe's Smoked Andouille Chicken Sausage (2 sausages)

1 teaspoon canola oil

2 cups chicken broth, or 2 cups hot water plus 2 (9.6-gram) pouches Trader Joe's Savory Chicken Concentrate

½ (15-ounce) can chickpeas, drained

1 (8-ounce) package Trader Joe's Cumin and Chili Chickpeas

1 tablespoon minced ginger

½ teaspoon kosher salt

½ teaspoon freshly ground black pepper

1 (6-ounce) bag baby spinach

The Trader Joe's Cumin and Chili Chickpeas are infused with so much garlic and spice goodness that they add a bolt of flavor to the soup.

1. Slice the sausages lengthwise and then cut each half into bite-size pieces.

2. In a large saucepan, heat the oil over medium-high heat until shimmering. Add the sausage and sauté until golden, 6 to 8 minutes, stirring occasionally. Remove the sausage from the pan and set aside.

3. In a medium pot, add the chicken broth, canned chickpeas, packaged chickpeas, ginger, salt, and pepper, and bring to a simmer over medium-high heat. Simmer for 5 to 8 minutes. Add the spinach and stir until it wilts, just a couple of minutes. Add the reserved sausage pieces and stir to combine.

EGG DROP SOUP *with* CILANTRO-CHICKEN WONTONS

YIELD: 2 servings
PREP TIME: 5 minutes
COOKING TIME: 15 minutes

3 cups chicken broth, or 3 cups hot water plus 3 (9.6-gram) pouches Trader Joe's Savory Chicken Concentrate

1 (16-ounce) bag frozen Trader Ming's Asian Vegetables with Beijing Style Soy Sauce

1 (12-ounce) bag frozen Trader Joe's Chicken Cilantro Mini Wontons

2 large eggs

kosher salt and freshly ground black pepper

Egg drop soup is one of those delightfully simple recipes that's so easy—once you know how to make it, you'll be preparing it all the time.

1. In a medium pot, bring the chicken broth to a boil over high heat.

2. Meanwhile, remove the soy sauce packet from the frozen vegetables and defrost it in the microwave until thawed, 1 to 2 minutes. Add the soy sauce packet to the chicken broth, stirring to combine. Once the broth is boiling, add the frozen vegetables. Reduce the heat to medium, and let the vegetables cook for 5 minutes. Add the mini wontons and cook for 2 to 3 minutes longer.

3. Meanwhile, crack the eggs into a small liquid measuring cup. Whisk the eggs with a fork until beaten.

4. Return the heat to high. When the broth is at a substantial boil, pour the beaten eggs in a thin, steady stream into the soup and stir the soup as the eggs hit the broth. Stir to combine. Season to taste with salt and pepper.

TURKEY *and* VEGETABLE CHILI

YIELD: 2 servings
PREP TIME: 5 minutes
COOKING TIME: 15 minutes

1 (12-ounce) package frozen Trader Joe's Turkey Bolognese

½ (1.3-ounce) packet Trader Joe's Taco Seasoning Mix

1 (13.4-ounce) jar Trader Joe's Ratatouille

1 (15.5-ounce) can pinto beans

¼ teaspoon kosher salt

¼ teaspoon freshly ground black pepper

Trader Joe's Salsa Tortilla Chips, as needed

OPTIONAL TOPPINGS: sour cream, grated cheese, salsa, pumpkinseeds

By using Trader Joe's Fully Cooked Turkey Bolognese and Trader Joe's Ratatouille, most of the work has already been done for you in this stew.

1. In a medium pot, add the turkey Bolognese and taco seasoning and stir to combine. Then add the ratatouille, pinto beans (liquid included), salt, and pepper. Bring to a boil over high heat. Then reduce the heat to low and let simmer for 10 minutes.
2. Ladle the chili into bowls and crumble tortilla chips on top. Serve with optional toppings, if using.

BEEF UDON SOUP

YIELD: 2 servings
PREP TIME: 10 minutes
COOKING TIME: 15 minutes

1 tablespoon canola oil

1 (10-ounce) bag sliced cremini mushrooms

3 cups beef broth

¼ teaspoon kosher salt, or more

¼ teaspoon freshly ground black pepper, or more

1 (10-ounce) container Trader Ming's Ginger Peanut Noodle Salad, gently chopped

½ pound Trader Joe's Shaved Beef Steak

Asian soups are always brimming with flavor, usually because of their long cooking times, but this beef udon soup provides an Asian soup fix in a snap.

1. In a medium pot, heat the oil over medium-high heat until shimmering. Add the mushrooms and sauté, stirring occasionally, until they begin to release their liquid, 5 to 8 minutes. Stir in the beef broth and increase the heat to high. Bring the broth to a boil, then add the salt and pepper.
2. Stir in the noodles. Carefully drop in the raw beef slices. Cook until the beef turns brown, about 1 minute. Remove the soup from the heat, taste, and adjust the seasonings with salt and pepper.

LOADED POTATO SOUP

YIELD: 2 servings
PREP TIME: 10 minutes
COOKING TIME: 15 to 20 minutes

½ (28-ounce) package frozen Trader Joe's Mashed Potatoes (about 25 medallions)

1 cup whole milk

2 cups chicken broth, or 2 cups hot water plus 2 (9.6-gram) pouches Trader Joe's Savory Chicken Concentrate

½ teaspoon kosher salt

¼ teaspoon freshly ground black pepper

8 slices Trader Joe's Fully Cooked Uncured Bacon

2 scallions, chopped

½ (8-ounce) package Trader Joe's Shredded Pepper Jack Cheese Blend

Similar to a loaded baked potato with all the fixings, except in a dreamy soup.

1. In a medium pot, add the potatoes, milk, chicken broth, salt, and pepper, and heat over medium-high heat, stirring every few minutes, until the potatoes have melted, 10 to 15 minutes.

2. Meanwhile, arrange the bacon slices between layers of paper towels in a small microwave-safe dish. Microwave on high until crispy, 30 to 45 seconds. Crumble the bacon into bits and combine with the scallions and cheese in a small bowl.

3. Once the potato soup is thick and bubbling, ladle into bowls. Generously top with the bacon and cheese mixture.

TOMATO-MEATBALL SOUP *with* CHEESE

YIELD: 2 servings
PREP TIME: 5 minutes
COOKING TIME: 15 minutes

Grilled cheese and tomato soup—this is the best of both worlds in one bowl.

1 (15-ounce) can Trader Joe's Organic Tomato Sauce

1 cup water

1 cup half-and-half

½ teaspoon kosher salt

¼ teaspoon freshly ground black pepper

½ (20-ounce) package Trader Joe's Party Size Mini Meatballs

½ loaf Trader Joe's Ciabatta

4 slices Swiss cheese

1. Preheat the oven's broiler.
2. In a medium pot, combine the tomato sauce, water, half-and-half, salt, and pepper, and bring to a boil over high heat. Reduce the heat to medium and simmer. Add the meatballs and cook until hot, 5 to 8 minutes.
3. Meanwhile, slice the bread lengthwise. Place the bread on a rimmed baking sheet and layer each half with 2 slices of cheese. Put the bread under the broiler to toast, 2 to 3 minutes, checking it about every 30 seconds.
4. Cut the bread into bite-size crouton pieces. Ladle the soup into bowls and top with the cheese croutons

Substitution: Milk can replace the half-and-half.

GAZPACHO

YIELD: 2 servings
PREP TIME: 5 minutes

In warmer months when you crave soup but may not be too keen on eating hot food, try gazpacho, an uncooked soup hailing from Spain.

½ (28-ounce) can Trader Joe's Whole Peeled and Salted Plum Tomatoes with Basil

1 (12-ounce) container Trader Joe's Tzatziki

juice of ½ lemon, or more

½ teaspoon kosher salt, or more

1. In a blender, add the tomatoes, tzatziki, lemon juice, and salt and blend on high speed until combined, 30 seconds to 1 minute. If you don't have a blender, place the tomatoes in a large bowl and use your hands to break them into pieces, then add the other ingredients.
2. Taste and adjust the seasoning with salt and lemon juice, as needed.
3. Serve at room temperature, or let the gazpacho chill in the fridge for 1 to 2 hours prior to serving.

CHAPTER 4

PASTAS

Pastas are among the easiest ways to quickly create a tasty dish. To this day when I'm short on time, I'll toss a batch of angel-hair pasta with butter and Parmesan cheese for a quick lunch or dinner that's easy, cheap, and—most essentially—tasty.

Of course, the first thing that pops into most people's heads when they think of pasta is a basic Italian red sauce, which you'll find in classic recipes like Spaghetti and Meatballs. The Italians may have mastered the art of pasta, but these recipes pull inspiration from all over the globe, using pasta to explore a wide array of flavor profiles, including those with a spark of Middle Eastern ingredients, like Chickpea Penne.

OLIVE OIL SPAGHETTI *with* ARUGULA

YIELD: 1 serving
PREP TIME: 5 minutes
COOKING TIME: 15 minutes

¼ (16-ounce package) Trader Giotto's Organic Spaghetti

1 tablespoon olive oil

¾ (12-ounce) container Trader Joe's Marinated Fresh Mozzarella, plus 3 to 4 tablespoons marinating oil

½ (7-ounce) bag arugula

½ teaspoon kosher salt

¼ teaspoon freshly ground black pepper

½ teaspoon red chile pepper flakes

In Italy, spaghetti aglio e olio *refers to spaghetti noodles tossed with olive oil, garlic, and crushed red pepper flakes. This is an easy twist, which replaces the garlic with a kick of arugula.*

1. Cook the spaghetti according to the package directions. Drain in a colander and toss with the olive oil.
2. Add 1 tablespoon marinade oil from the mozzarella to the now empty pot and heat over medium-high heat until shimmering. Add the arugula, stirring constantly, until it wilts, 2 to 3 minutes. Remove from the heat.
3. Add the pasta to the pot along with the salt, pepper, chile pepper flakes, mozzarella, and 2 to 3 tablespoons marinade oil. Toss to combine.

CHICKPEA PENNE

YIELD: 2 servings
PREP TIME: 1 minute
COOKING TIME: 10 minutes

½ (16-ounce) package frozen Trader Joe's "Just Pasta" Penne

1 (10-ounce) package Trader Joe's Channa Masala

½ teaspoon Trader Joe's Crushed Garlic

Easiest. Pasta. Ever. The Trader Joe's Channa Masala is a mix of tomatoes, chickpeas, and spices, which adds a Middle Eastern flair.

1. Microwave the pasta according to the package directions.
2. Pierce a few holes in the plastic film on the channa masala. Microwave on high power until warm, 4 to 4½ minutes.
3. Transfer the pasta to a medium bowl. Add the channa masala and the garlic. Stir to combine.

EGGPLANT PARMESAN SPAGHETTI

YIELD: 2 servings
PREP TIME: 5 minutes
COOKING TIME: 20 minutes

½ (16-ounce) package Trader Giotto's Organic Spaghetti

1 tablespoon olive oil

1½ cups Trader Giotto's Roasted Garlic Spaghetti Sauce

1 (12-ounce) box frozen Trader Joe's Stacked Eggplant Parmesan, defrosted

½ teaspoon kosher salt

¼ teaspoon freshly ground black pepper

Trader Joe's Eggplant Parmesan is transformed into delicious tomato pasta studded with breaded bits of eggplant.

1. Cook the spaghetti according to the package directions. Drain and toss with the olive oil.
2. Heat the marinara sauce in a medium skillet over medium-high heat. Cut each eggplant piece into quarters. Add the contents of the eggplant Parmesan to the skillet, along with the salt and pepper. Stir to combine and cook until hot, about 5 minutes.
3. Add the pasta to the pan and gently toss to combine.

EGGPLANT AND GARLIC CAPELLINI

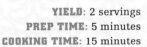

YIELD: 2 servings
PREP TIME: 5 minutes
COOKING TIME: 15 minutes

½ (16-ounce) package Trader Joe's Italian Capellini

1 tablespoon plus 1 teaspoon olive oil

2 medium tomatoes, diced

1 (12-ounce) jar Trader Joe's Eggplant Garlic Spread

juice of 1 lemon

½ teaspoon kosher salt

¼ teaspoon freshly ground black pepper

The Bulgarian-style Trader Joe's Eggplant Garlic Spread is a tasty base for this Mediterranean-inspired pasta.

1. Cook the capellini according to the package directions. Reserve ⅓ cup pasta water, then drain the pasta and toss with 1 tablespoon olive oil.
2. In a medium skillet, warm the remaining 1 teaspoon olive oil over medium-high heat until shimmering. Add the tomatoes and sauté just a few minutes, stirring constantly, until the tomatoes are cooked. Add the eggplant spread, lemon juice, reserved pasta water, salt, and pepper and stir to combine. Reduce the heat to medium-low and simmer for 5 minutes.
3. Add the pasta to the skillet and toss to coat with the sauce.

PORTABELLA MUSHROOM RAVIOLI

YIELD: 2 servings
PREP TIME: 5 minutes
COOKING TIME: 10 minutes

2 (9-ounce) packages Trader Joe's Chunky Portabella Mushroom Ravioli

1 tablespoon olive oil

2 teaspoons Trader Joe's Crushed Garlic

2 tablespoons Trader Joe's Coastal Sauvignon Blanc, or any other dry white wine

⅓ cup chicken broth

1 tablespoon unsalted butter

½ teaspoon kosher salt

¼ teaspoon freshly ground black pepper

Trader Joe's Grated Parmigiano-Reggiano cheese, as needed (optional)

These ravioli stuffed with mushrooms and provolone cheese have so much flavor that they need only a minimal coating in this light sauce.

1. Cook the ravioli according to the package directions. Drain.

2. In a medium skillet over high heat, heat the olive oil until shimmering. Add the garlic and cook for 15 to 30 seconds. Add the wine, chicken broth, butter, salt, and pepper to the pan, stirring and cooking until the butter melts.

3. Add the ravioli to the sauce, remove from the heat, and carefully toss to combine. Top with cheese, if using.

FARFALLE *with* VODKA SAUCE

YIELD: 2 servings
PREP TIME: 5 minutes
COOKING TIME: 15 minutes

½ (16-ounce) package Trader Joe's Farfalle Pasta

1½ tablespoons olive oil, divided

2½ ounces basil, leaves plucked from stem

½ (25-ounce) Trader Giotto's Organic Vodka Sauce

1 cup Trader Giotto's Traditional Fresh Ricotta

Farfalle pasta resembles butterflies or bow ties, so it's often paired with chunkier sauces.

1. Cook the farfalle according to the package directions. Drain and toss with 1 tablespoon olive oil.
2. In the pot used for the pasta, warm the remaining ½ tablespoon olive oil over medium-high heat until shimmering. Add the basil and stir until the basil is wilted, 30 seconds to 1 minute.
3. Add the vodka sauce to the pot and stir to combine. Let the sauce cook until hot, just a few minutes. Remove the pot from the heat. Stir in the ricotta and pasta.

SPAGHETTI PUTTANESCA

YIELD: 2 servings
PREP TIME: 5 minutes
COOKING TIME: 15 minutes

½ (16-ounce) package Trader Giotto's Organic Spaghetti

1 tablespoon olive oil

1 (15-ounce) can Trader Joe's Organic Tomato Sauce

¼ (4.25-ounce) tin Trader Joe's Lightly Smoked Sardines in Olive Oil

2 teaspoons Trader Joe's Crushed Garlic

2 tablespoons Trader Joe's Olive Tapenade Spread

1 tablespoon capers, rinsed and chopped

Puttanesca is an Italian tomato sauce with tomatoes, capers, olives, anchovies, and garlic. Here, delicate smoked sardines fill in for the harsher taste of anchovies.

1. Cook the spaghetti according to the package directions. Reserve ½ cup pasta water, then drain the pasta and toss with the olive oil.
2. In a medium pot, add the tomato sauce, reserved pasta water, sardines, garlic, tapenade, and capers. Cook over medium heat, stirring frequently. Let simmer for 10 minutes.
3. Add the pasta and toss to combine.

CAPELLINI *with* SMOKED SARDINES, GARLIC, *and* PINE NUTS

YIELD: 2 servings
PREP TIME: 5 minutes
COOKING TIME: 12 minutes

½ (16-ounce) package Trader Joe's Italian Capellini

2 tablespoons olive oil, divided

1 (4.25-ounce) tin Trader Joe's Lightly Smoked Sardines in Olive Oil

½ teaspoon kosher salt

¼ teaspoon freshly ground black pepper

1 teaspoon Trader Joe's Crushed Garlic

2 tablespoons Trader Joe's Dry Roasted Pignolias (pine nuts, see page 154)

Capellini is one of my favorite pastas to use because of the amazingly quick cooking time.

1. Cook the capellini according to the package directions. Drain and toss with 1 tablespoon olive oil.

2. In a medium skillet, heat the sardines and 1 tablespoon olive oil over medium-high heat. Use a spatula to break up the sardines and combine them with the oil. When the sardines have melded with the oil, add the salt, pepper, garlic, and pine nuts. Cook, stirring constantly, until the garlic and pine nuts are golden, 1 to 2 minutes.

3. Remove from the heat, add the pasta to the sauce, and toss well.

SEAFOOD FETTUCCINI

YIELD: 2 servings
PREP TIME: 5 minutes
COOKING TIME: 15 minutes

¼ (16-ounce) package Trader Joe's Organic Whole Wheat Fettuccini

2 tablespoons olive oil, divided

½ (16-ounce) package Trader Joe's Seafood Blend, thawed

½ cup white wine

2 tablespoons unsalted butter

2 cubes frozen parsley

Trader Joe's Frozen Seafood Blend—a mix of shrimp, calamari, and bay scallops—is an affordable way to get a wide array of seafood into your diet.

1. Cook the fettuccini according to the package directions. Drain and toss with 1 tablespoon olive oil.
2. In a medium skillet, heat the remaining 1 tablespoon olive oil over medium-high heat until shimmering. Add the defrosted seafood mix and cook 1 to 2 minutes, being sure the seafood does not overcook. Add the white wine, butter, and parsley, cooking until the butter melts, just 30 seconds to 1 minute.
3. Remove the pan from the heat, add the pasta, and toss to combine.

SPINACH ALFREDO LINGUINE *with* CHICKEN

YIELD: 3 servings
PREP TIME: 5 minutes
COOKING TIME: 15 minutes

½ (16-ounce) package frozen chopped spinach

1 (8-ounce) package Trader Joe's Spinach and Chive Linguine Pasta

1 tablespoon olive oil

1 (16.9-ounce) jar Trader Giotto's Alfredo Pasta Sauce

½ (12-ounce) package Trader Joe's Grilled Lemon Pepper Chicken

Trader Joe's Grated Parmigiano-Reggiano cheese, as needed (optional)

Creamy Alfredo sauce melds with spinach linguine and chopped spinach for double the spinach power.

1. In a small colander, run cold water over the spinach until thawed, 3 to 4 minutes, then squeeze it to remove excess water.
2. Cook the pasta according to the package directions. Drain, rinse with cold water, and toss with the olive oil.
3. In the pot used for the pasta, heat the Alfredo sauce over medium-high heat. Toss in the spinach, stirring to make sure it's well combined with the sauce. Add the chicken and cook until hot.
4. Add the pasta and toss to combine. Top with cheese, if desired.

SPAGHETTI *and* MEATBALLS

YIELD: 2 servings
PREP TIME: 5 minutes
COOKING TIME: 15 minutes

¼ (16-ounce package) Trader Giotto's Organic Spaghetti

1 tablespoon olive oil

½ (25-ounce) jar Trader Giotto's Organic Tomato Basil Marinara

3 tablespoons unsalted butter, cut into pieces

½ (16-ounce) package frozen Trader Joe's Flame Broiled Turkey Meatballs Fully Cooked

2 to 3 tablespoons Trader Joe's Grated Parmigiano-Reggiano cheese (optional)

Trader Joe's Flame Broiled Turkey Meatballs add a grilled flavor to this traditional dish.

1. Cook the spaghetti according to the package directions. Drain and toss with the olive oil.
2. In a medium skillet, heat the marinara sauce over medium-high heat. Once it's bubbling, reduce the heat to low and simmer. Add the butter pieces and stir.
3. Microwave the meatballs according to the package directions. Add the meatballs to the sauce and stir. Simmer for 5 minutes. Remove the pot from the heat, add the pasta, and toss to combine. Top with cheese, if using.

ROTELLE *with* PESTO, PEAS, *and* PROSCIUTTO

YIELD: 2 servings
PREP TIME: 5 minutes
COOKING TIME: 15 minutes

½ (16-ounce) package Trader Joe's Organic Whole Wheat Rotelle Pasta

½ (16-ounce) bag Trader Joe's Petite Peas

½ (4-ounce) package Trader Joe's Sliced Prosciutto

1 (6.7-ounce) jar Trader Giotto's Pesto alla Genovese (basil pesto)

¼ teaspoon freshly ground black pepper

Because both the pesto and prosciutto are relatively salty, taste the pasta before adding any salt.

1. Bring a medium pot of salted water to a boil over high heat. Add the rotelle to the water and cook for 8 minutes. Add the peas to the boiling water with the pasta and cook until the pasta is al dente (see page 153), about 2 minutes longer. Reserve ½ cup pasta water, then drain the pasta and peas in a colander.
2. Shred the prosciutto into bite-size pieces.
3. Transfer the pasta and peas back to the pot and add the pesto, reserved pasta water, and pepper. Stir constantly to let the pesto incorporate with the pasta and peas. Warm over low heat, as needed. Top with the shredded prosciutto.

SPAGHETTI *with* CHICKEN SAUSAGE *and* TOMATO SAUCE

YIELD: 2 servings
PREP TIME: 10 minutes
COOKING TIME: 40 minutes

½ (28-ounce) can Trader Joe's Plum Tomatoes with Basil

2 tablespoons olive oil, divided

1 small or medium onion, diced (see page 153)

½ (12-ounce) package fully cooked Trader Joe's Spicy Italian Chicken Sausage (2 sausages), sliced into ½-inch rounds

1 cube frozen basil

½ teaspoon freshly ground black pepper

1 teaspoon white vinegar or lemon juice

6 ounces Trader Giotto's Organic Spaghetti

A quick, basic tomato sauce should be in everyone's cooking arsenal. The spicy Italian sausage is an easy addition that makes this feel like a full meal.

1. Pour the tomatoes into a bowl and break the whole tomatoes into 2 to 3 pieces each.
2. Heat 1 tablespoon oil in a medium skillet over medium heat until shimmering, then add the onion and cook for 30 to 45 seconds, stirring constantly to prevent burning. Add the tomatoes and their liquid, and the sausage, basil, pepper, and vinegar. Bring to a boil, then reduce heat to low, cover the pan, and simmer until the flavors have combined, 20 to 30 minutes.
3. Meanwhile, cook the spaghetti according to the package directions. Drain and toss with the remaining 1 tablespoon olive oil. Add the pasta to the sauce and toss to combine.

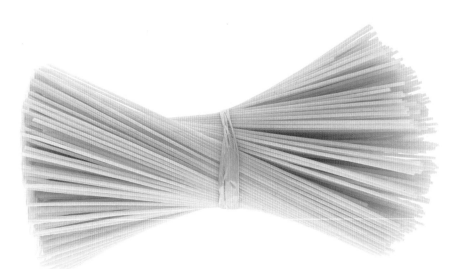

MAIN MEALS

Y ou've had a long day full of sleep-inducing lectures and handed-in assignments. At the end of the night, you crave a good meal that's low on hassle. Well, you're in luck. With step-by-step instructions and Trader Joe's products, whipping up warm homemade meals can be done on the cheap and with ease. There's no need to survive on ramen noodles night after night. Cook chicken thighs in tomatillo salsa and eat them with tortillas, or sauté pork chops and top them with a creamy spinach sauce. A delicious dinner is just minutes away.

FISH TACOS *with* MANGO SALSA

YIELD: 4 tacos
PREP TIME: 5 minutes
COOKING TIME: 10 minutes

2 fillets frozen Trader Joe's Panko Breaded Tilapia Fillets

½ mango, diced

½ cup Trader Joe's Corn and Chile Tomato-Less Salsa

4 corn or flour tortillas

cilantro sprigs (optional)

The sweetness of Trader Joe's Corn and Chile Salsa begs for a fruitlicious pairing like mango.

1. Preheat the oven to 425°F. Line a rimmed baking sheet with foil.
2. Place the fish fillets on the prepared baking sheet and bake until hot, 20 to 25 minutes.
3. In a small bowl, stir together the mango and corn salsa.
4. Cut the fish into strips. Layer the fish strips onto the tortillas, garnishing with the mango and corn salsa and cilantro sprigs.

CHICKEN *in* TOMATILLO SAUCE

YIELD: 2 servings
PREP TIME: 5 minutes
COOKING TIME: 30 minutes

1 (12-ounce) jar Trader Joe's Salsa Verde

1 (12-ounce) container Trader Joe's Salsa Verde Autentica

2 to 3 pieces frozen Trader Joe's Boneless Skinless Chicken Thigh Meat

½ teaspoon kosher salt

¼ teaspoon freshly ground black pepper

Trader Joe's Authentic Tortillas

This recipe uses two kinds of Trader Joe's tomatillo sauce. The jarred salsa verde is tangier, while the refrigerated autentica version is chunkier.

1. In a medium pot, add the salsa verde, salsa verde autentica, chicken, salt, and pepper. Stir to combine.
2. Heat the mixture over high heat until the liquid boils. Cover and reduce the heat to low. Simmer until the chicken is cooked through, 25 to 30 minutes. Cut into the thickest chicken piece to determine it's no longer pink.
3. Remove the chicken from the tomatillo sauce and cut it into pieces. Return the chicken to the sauce. Serve with tortillas.

TUNA CASSEROLE

YIELD: 2 servings
PREP TIME: 10 minutes
COOKING TIME: 25 minutes

1 tablespoon canola oil

celery and onions from
1 (14.5-ounce) container Trader
Joe's Mirepoix

½ teaspoon kosher salt

2 Trader Joe's Fire-Roasted Red
and Yellow Peppers, cut into
bite-size pieces

2 (5-ounce) cans Trader Joe's
Albacore Solid White Tuna
in Water

½ cup mayonnaise

½ cup Trader Joe's Japanese-
Style Panko Bread Crumbs

This one-skillet wonder is based on a tuna casserole recipe my mom made for me growing up. It continues to be one of my favorite dishes.

1. Preheat the oven to 350°F.
2. In a medium oven-safe skillet, heat the oil over medium-high heat until shimmering. Add the celery and onions and sauté until the vegetables are soft, 4 to 5 minutes.
3. Remove the pan from the heat. Add the salt, peppers, tuna, and mayonnaise, stirring to combine. Top the casserole with bread crumbs. Bake until the tuna is hot throughout, 15 to 20 minutes.

CHICKEN MASALA *with* SWEET POTATOES

YIELD: 2 servings
PREP TIME: 5 minutes
COOKING TIME: 30 minutes

1 (15-ounce) jar Trader Joe's
Masala Simmer Sauce

½ cup water

2 pieces frozen Trader Joe's
Boneless Skinless Chicken Thigh
Meat

½ teaspoon kosher salt

¼ teaspoon freshly ground black
pepper

1 (12-ounce) bag Trader Joe's
Sweet Potato Spears

Trader Joe's Garlic Naan Bread
(frozen) or rice

Trader Joe's Masala Simmer Sauce is inspired by the typical preparation of chicken tikka masala, which has a tomato base and mild Indian spices.

1. In a medium pot, combine the masala simmer sauce, water, chicken, salt, and pepper. Heat the mixture over high heat until it boils, then cover the pot and reduce the heat to low. Cook for 15 minutes.
2. Meanwhile, coarsely chop the sweet potato into bite-size pieces. Stir the sweet potatoes into the sauce. Cover the pot and cook an additional 15 minutes.
3. Remove the pot from the heat. Cut into the thickest chicken piece to determine it's no longer pink. Serve with naan bread or rice.

GARLIC BUTTER SHRIMP *with* QUINOA

YIELD: 2 servings
PREP TIME: 5 minutes
COOKING TIME: 7 minutes

½ (16-ounce) package
Trader Joe's Quinoa Duo with
Vegetable Medley

3 tablespoons unsalted butter

1 tablespoon Trader Joe's
Crushed Garlic

½ teaspoon kosher salt

¼ teaspoon freshly ground black
pepper

½ pound Trader Joe's Jumbo
Cooked Shrimp (to use raw
shrimp, see page 154)

Pairing the super-tasty shrimp, butter, and garlic trio with quinoa, a grainlike seed packed with amino acids, protein, and other nutrients, makes this a healthy dinner.

1. Microwave the quinoa and vegetables in a large dish according to the package directions.
2. In a medium skillet over medium-high, melt the butter, then add the garlic, salt, and pepper and cook for just 30 seconds. Add the cooked shrimp and stir to coat it in the sauce just until hot, about 30 seconds.
3. Pour the shrimp and sauce over the quinoa and vegetables.

CHICKEN *and* CHEESE ENCHILADAS

YIELD: 4 to 6 enchiladas
PREP TIME: 15 minutes
COOKING TIME: 25 minutes

½ (16-ounce) package Trader
Joe's Just Chicken white meat

1 (12-ounce) bottle Trader Joe's
Enchilada Sauce, divided

½ teaspoon kosher salt

¼ teaspoon freshly ground black
pepper

1½ cups shredded cheese, such
as Trader Joe's Fancy Shredded
Lite Mexican Blend, divided

½ cup sour cream

4 to 6 whole wheat
flour tortillas

Add a little cayenne pepper into the mix if you want to kick up the spiciness of these enchiladas.

1. Preheat the oven to 400°F. Spray a baking dish with cooking spray.
2. Chop the chicken into very small pieces and place in a medium bowl with three-quarters of the enchilada sauce, the salt, pepper, 1 cup shredded cheese, and sour cream. Stir to combine the enchilada filling.
3. Spoon the filling down the center of each tortilla, dividing it evenly among the tortillas, and roll the enchiladas up.
4. Arrange the enchiladas in the prepared baking dish. Drizzle the remaining sauce over the enchiladas.
5. Bake until the enchiladas are hot throughout, 20 to 25 minutes. Garnish with the remaining cheese.

MAIN MEALS **69**

MEDITERRANEAN CHICKEN *with* FETA CHEESE *and* SUN DRIED TOMATOES

YIELD: 2 servings
PREP TIME: 5 minutes
COOKING TIME: 6 minutes

1 pound Trader Joe's Organic Free Range Chicken Breast Tenders

½ teaspoon kosher salt

¼ teaspoon freshly ground black pepper

1 tablespoon canola oil

½ cup Trader Joe's Julienne Sliced Sun Dried Tomatoes in Olive Oil, plus 1 tablespoon of the oil

¼ cup pitted kalamata olives

½ cup Trader Joe's Crumbled Feta with Mediterranean Herbs

This dish is easy enough to make for yourself on a weekly basis, but flavorful and colorful enough to serve on a special occasion.

1. Season the chicken with salt and pepper. In a medium skillet, heat the oil over medium-high heat until shimmering. Add the chicken and sauté until golden on one side, 2 to 3 minutes. Flip the chicken over and cook for 2 to 3 minutes longer. Cut into the thickest piece to determine it's no longer pink.

2. In a small bowl, stir the sun dried tomatoes with the olives and feta to combine.

3. Transfer the chicken to a serving plate and top with the feta mixture.

PORK CHOPS *in* CREAMY SPINACH SAUCE

YIELD: 2 servings
PREP TIME: 5 minutes
COOKING TIME: 10 minutes

1 package (about 1 pound) Trader Joe's Bone-in Frenched Center Cut Pork Chops

½ teaspoon kosher salt

¼ teaspoon freshly ground black pepper

1 tablespoon canola oil

½ (8.8-ounce) container frozen Trader Joe's Creamy Spinach and Artichoke Dip

2 tablespoons heavy cream

This recipe uses Frenched pork chops, which are rib chops from which the meat and fat have been trimmed from the end of the bone.

1. Pat the pork chops dry with a paper towel and season them with salt and pepper.

2. In a large heavy skillet, heat the oil over medium-high heat until shimmering. Carefully add the pork chops and sauté until browned and golden on each side, about 4 minutes per side.

3. Remove the pan from the heat and transfer the pork chops to a cutting board. Cut into one of the pork chops to determine it's no longer pink. Cover loosely with foil.

4. In a microwave-safe dish, add the spinach dip, cheese-side up. Microwave on high for 2 minutes.

5. Stir the heavy cream into the spinach dip and microwave on high for 2 minutes longer. Transfer the pork chops to plates and pour the spinach sauce over the meat.

ASIAN MEATBALLS *in* PEANUT SAUCE

YIELD: 3 servings
PREP TIME: 15 minutes
COOKING TIME: 20 minutes

½ pound ground pork

½ (8-ounce) can water chestnuts, finely chopped

1 tablespoon minced ginger

1 large egg

½ teaspoon kosher salt

¼ teaspoon freshly ground black pepper

¼ cup Trader Joe's Japanese-Style Panko Bread Crumbs

½ (16-ounce) package Trader Joe's Italian Capellini

1 (9-ounce) jar Trader Joe's Satay Peanut Sauce

2 tablespoons chopped scallions

These Asian-flavored pork meatballs are paired with thin capellini noodles and a Thai peanut sauce, resulting in an Asian riff on spaghetti and meatballs.

1. Preheat the oven to 425°F. Spray a rimmed baking sheet with cooking spray.

2. In a large bowl, combine the ground pork, water chestnuts, ginger, egg, salt, pepper, and bread crumbs with your hands.

3. Roll about 1 tablespoon of the meat mixture into meatballs one at a time and place on the prepared baking sheet. Bake until cooked through, 12 to 15 minutes. Cut into a meatball to determine that it's no longer pink.

4. Meanwhile, cook the capellini according to the package directions. Drain the pasta in a colander and return to the pot. Add the peanut sauce and scallions to the pasta and cook over medium heat, stirring constantly, just 1 to 2 minutes. Portion pasta and sauce onto plates, top with meatballs, and serve.

SOYAKI STEAK

YIELD: 2 servings
PREP TIME: 5 minutes active, plus 1 hour for marinating
COOKING TIME: 6 to 10 minutes, depending on desired doneness of steak

1 Trader Joe's Butcher Shop Boneless Beef Rib Eye Steak (about 1 pound)

1 cup Trader Joe's Island Soyaki

kosher salt and freshly ground black pepper

Trader Joe's Island Soyaki includes pineapple juice, which contains bromelain, a natural enzyme known to tenderize meat.

1. In a shallow dish, cover the steak with the Soyaki. Marinate for at least 1 hour in the refrigerator.
2. Remove the steak from the marinade and discard the marinade. Dab the steak with a paper towel to remove the marinade.
3. Preheat the oven's broiler. Line a rimmed baking sheet with foil.
4. Place the steak on the prepared baking sheet and season it with salt and pepper. Cook the steak under the broiler 2 to 3 minutes per side, until it reaches your desired doneness (see page 153). You may need to make a cut into the center of the steak to determine its doneness.
5. Remove the steak from the oven, transfer to a cutting board, and cover with a piece of foil. Let the steak rest for 5 minutes before slicing and serving.

BEEF STROGANOFF WANNABE

YIELD: 2 servings
PREP TIME: 5 minutes
COOKING TIME: 18 minutes

1 (10-ounce) package sliced white mushrooms

½ tablespoon canola oil

½ (16-ounce) package Trader Joe's Italian Fusilli

½ (16-ounce) package Trader Joe's Traditional Pot Roast, cut into bite-size pieces

1 (11-ounce) box Trader Joe's Condensed Cream of Portabella Mushroom Soup

½ teaspoon kosher salt

½ teaspoon freshly ground black pepper

1 cup sour cream

2 tablespoons chopped chives (optional)

Trader Joe's Condensed Cream of Portabella Soup infuses beefy noodles with that earthy mushroom taste.

1. Cut the larger mushrooms in half so all the slices are similar in size.
2. In a medium skillet, heat the oil over medium-high heat until shimmering. Add the mushrooms and cook until softened, about 10 minutes, stirring occasionally.
3. Cook the fusilli according to the package directions and drain.
4. Increase the heat to high and add the pot roast pieces to the mushrooms, mixing the mushrooms and beef together and cooking just 1 minute. Add the portabella soup, salt, and pepper. Cook until the sauce is bubbling, 2 to 3 minutes, stirring occasionally.
5. Remove from the heat and stir in the sour cream. Toss with the pasta. Garnish with chives, if using.

BACON CHEESEBURGER

YIELD: 4 burgers
PREP TIME: 10 minutes
COOKING TIME: 6 minutes

1 (1-pound) package Trader Joe's Organic Ground Beef

2 teaspoons Trader Joe's Everyday Seasoning with Grinder

2 teaspoons canola oil

4 slices Trader Joe's Fully Cooked Uncured Bacon (about 4 slices)

4 Trader Joe's Honey Wheat Hamburger Buns

4 slices American cheese or your favorite kind

OPTIONAL CONDIMENTS AND TOPPINGS:
ketchup, mustard, lettuce, tomato, avocado, onions, salsa

This is a good basic hamburger recipe—you're free to use any toppings you like.

1. Place the ground beef in a medium bowl and grind the everyday seasoning onto the meat and combine. Mold the meat into 4 patties.
2. In a medium skillet, heat the oil over medium-high heat until shimmering. Add the hamburger patties to the pan and cook until both burger sides are browned and have reached the desired doneness in the center (see page 153), about 3 minutes on each side, making sure to press the burgers down with a spatula when flipping them.
3. Meanwhile, arrange the bacon slices between layers of paper towels in a small microwave-safe dish. Microwave on high until crispy, 30 to 45 seconds. Warm the buns in the microwave.
4. Top each burger with a slice of cheese. Transfer the cheeseburgers to the buns and top with the bacon and other desired condiments.

SLOPPY JOES

YIELD: 3 to 4 servings
PREP TIME: 5 minutes
COOKING TIME: 10 minutes

1 teaspoon canola oil

1 pound Trader Joe's Butcher Shop Ground Beef 80/20

½ teaspoon kosher salt

¼ teaspoon freshly ground black pepper

½ cup ketchup

2 tablespoons yellow mustard

2 tablespoons honey

3 to 4 Trader Joe's Honey Wheat Hamburger Buns

When I was a kid, sloppy joes were my go-to birthday meal request.

1. In a medium skillet, heat the oil over medium-high heat until shimmering. Add the ground beef, salt, and pepper, stirring every couple of minutes to break up the meat. Sauté the meat until fully cooked, 6 to 7 minutes.

2. Take the pan off the heat. Push the cooked meat to one side of the pan and remove and discard most of the fat.

3. Stir the ketchup, mustard, and honey into the beef and heat the mixture over medium-high heat until the beef is hot and combined with the sauce. Remove from the heat and cover, to keep hot. Microwave the buns until warm. Pile the meat mixture onto the buns.

Note: The term "80/20" refers to the percentage of fat contained in the meat: 80/20 beef has 20 percent fat and is considered 80 percent lean.

TOSTADAS

YIELD: 3 tostadas
PREP TIME: 5 minutes
COOKING TIME: 12 minutes

½ (12-ounce) package frozen Trader Joe's Carne Asada (seasoned beef sirloin)

½ (15-ounce) can Trader Joe's Refried Black Beans with Jalapeño Peppers

½ (8-ounce) package Trader Joe's Shredded Pepper Jack Cheese Blend

canola oil, as needed

3 flour tortillas

½ (16-ounce) container Trader José's Guacamole Topped with Spicy Pico de Gallo

OPTIONAL TOPPINGS:
chopped tomatoes, shredded lettuce, sour cream, salsa

Freshly fried to a golden crisp, tostadas are crunchy, slightly greasy (in a good way), and downright delicious.

1. Line a plate with a paper towel. Microwave the carne asada and refried beans on high for 2 to 3 minutes, stirring occasionally. Remove from the microwave and top with the cheese.

2. In a large skillet, heat 1 inch of oil over high heat until shimmering. Add 1 tortilla and fry until golden on each side, about 2 minutes per side. Transfer to the prepared plate to drain. Repeat with the remaining tortillas.

3. Layer the tostadas with the hot meat and bean mixture and top with guacamole and pico de gallo and other desired toppings.

MEAT LOAF MUFFINS

YIELD: 8 meat loaf muffins
PREP TIME: 20 minutes
COOKING TIME: 30 minutes

½ cup Trader Joe's Cheese and Garlic Croutons

¾ pound Trader Joe's Butcher Shop Ground Beef 96/4

1 cup frozen Trader Joe's Fire Roasted Bell Pepper and Onions, thawed

1 teaspoon kosher salt

½ teaspoon freshly ground black pepper

1 large egg

2 tablespoons ketchup

½ cup Trader Joe's Hot and Sweet Mustard

Making meat loaf into muffins not only makes it cuter, it greatly shortens the cooking time.

1. Preheat the oven to 350°F. Spray 8 muffin cups with cooking spray.
2. Seal the croutons into a plastic bag and pound into crumbs. In a large bowl, mix the crumbs, ground beef, pepper and onions, salt, pepper, egg, and ketchup.
3. Pack the meat mixture into as many prepared muffin cups as possible until almost full but not overflowing. Pour water into any empty cups to prevent scorching. Bake for 15 minutes. Remove the pan from the oven and glaze each meat loaf with the mustard.
4. Return the pan to the oven and cook for an additional 15 minutes. Cut into one meat loaf to make sure it's no longer pink. Cool for a few minutes.

VEGETARIAN MAIN MEALS

Even if you're a massive carnivore, vegetarian meals should be slowly woven into your diet (and take this from a total carnivore herself). One good reason is that meat—even with Trader Joe's meat at drastically affordable prices—is more expensive to consume. Meals with veggies, beans, and/or soy products are going to be more affordable.

TAQUITO CASSEROLE

YIELD: 2 servings
PREP TIME: 10 minutes
COOKING TIME: 25 minutes

Trader Joe's thin black bean–stuffed taquitos are piled on top of each other and blended with sour cream, salsa, and cheese.

1 (16-ounce) package Trader José's Black Bean and Cheese Taquitos (12 pieces)

1 cup sour cream

¾ cup Trader Joe's Organic Tomatillo and Roasted Yellow Chili Salsa

½ (11.5-ounce) jar Trader Joe's Queso Cheese Dip

1. Preheat the oven to 400°F. In a small baking dish, lay half the taquitos side by side.
2. In a small bowl, mix the sour cream and salsa together. Pour the sauce over the taquitos and layer the remaining taquitos on top. Top the second layer of taquitos with the queso dip.
3. Bake until hot, 20 to 25 minutes.

TERIYAKI TOFU *with* BABY BROCCOLI

YIELD: 2 servings
PREP TIME: 10 minutes active
COOKING TIME: 10 minutes

Tofu doesn't have a ton of flavor, which is why it's good to let it marinate in Trader Joe San Soyaki to give it a great taste for this filling vegan meal.

½ (14-ounce) package Trader Joe's Firm Organic Tofu, cut into ½-inch cubes

½ (21-ounce) bottle Trader Joe San Soyaki

1 tablespoon canola oil

1 (8-ounce) package Trader Joe's Organic Baby Broccoli, cut into 1-inch pieces

1 Trader Joe's Fire Roasted Red Pepper (from a jar), cut into bite-size pieces

1 (10-ounce) package Trader Joe's Thai-Style Lime Pilaf Fully Cooked with Coconut Milk and Lemon Grass

1. In a medium bowl, cover the tofu cubes with the Soyaki and let marinate for at least 30 minutes. When ready to use, drain the tofu, reserving ⅓ cup of the marinade.
2. Heat the oil in a large skillet over medium heat until shimmering. Add the broccoli, red pepper, and tofu and sauté about 5 minutes. Add the reserved marinade and cook until broccoli is fully cooked, about 5 minutes, stirring occasionally.
3. Microwave the rice according to the package directions. Scoop the rice into bowls and top with the tofu mixture.

TACO TIME

YIELD: 2 servings
PREP TIME: 5 minutes
COOKING TIME: 5 minutes

1 (8-ounce) package Trader Joe's
Chicken-less Strips

½ (16-ounce) can Trader Joe's
Vegetarian Refried Pinto Beans
Salsa Style

½ cup Trader Joe's Shredded
Smoked Cheese Blend

½ (5.5-ounce) package Trader
José's Taco Shells

½ cup Trader Joe's Corn and
Chile Tomato-Less Salsa

¼ (16-ounce) bag Trader Joe's
Very American Salad

2 Roma tomatoes, chopped

This has all the ingredients that make for a vegetarian version of a classic taco, including Trader Joe's Chicken-less Strips.

1. In a medium microwave-safe dish, place the chicken-less strips and the pinto beans. Microwave on high until hot, 2 to 3 minutes, stirring halfway through. Top with the cheese and microwave on high until melted, about 30 seconds.
2. Pile the mixture into the taco shells. Garnish with the salsa, salad, and tomatoes.

CURRIED CAULIFLOWER

YIELD: 2 servings
PREP TIME: 5 minutes
COOKING TIME: 6 minutes

2 (12-ounce) bags cauliflower florets

1 (15-ounce) jar Trader Joe's Curry Simmer Sauce

1 (10.5-ounce) package Trader Joe's Brown Rice Fully Cooked

I've long thought that cauliflower is an underappreciated vegetable. Its subtle flavor works well with the greater intensity of the dairy-free Curry Simmer Sauce.

1. Snip off the top corners of the cauliflower packets and microwave on high for 1 minute. In a large microwave-safe dish, place the curry sauce and the cauliflower and microwave on high until hot, about 2 to 3 minutes, stirring halfway through.
2. Cook the rice in the microwave according to the package directions.
3. Stir the rice into the cauliflower and curry sauce.

STUFFED BAKED POTATOES

YIELD: 2 servings
PREP TIME: 10 minutes
COOKING TIME: 1 hour

2 russet potatoes

½ (8.8-ounce) container frozen Trader Joe's Creamy Spinach and Artichoke Dip

1 tablespoon unsalted butter

kosher salt and freshly ground black pepper

Don't let the long cooking time in this recipe scare you— all of it is unattended. Just pop the potatoes into the oven and let it do all the work.

1. Preheat the oven to 400°F.
2. Using a fork, poke numerous holes into the potatoes and place them on a rimmed baking sheet. Bake until a knife can be inserted into a potato without any resistance, about 1 hour. Let the potatoes cool for about 10 minutes.
3. Meanwhile, in a microwave-safe dish, place the dip, cheese-side up. Microwave on high for 2 minutes. Stir and cook 2 minutes longer.
4. Slice halfway through the center of each potato, lengthwise. Add ½ tablespoon butter to each potato and season to taste with salt and pepper. Pour the hot dip over each potato.

BRIE *and* BUTTERNUT SQUASH QUESADILLAS

YIELD: 2 quesadillas
PREP TIME: 5 minutes
COOKING TIME: 12 minutes

1 (12-ounce) bag Trader Joe's Cut Butternut Squash

1 tablespoon brown sugar

¼ teaspoon kosher salt

¼ teaspoon freshly ground black pepper

½ wedge Trader Joe's Double Cream Brie

2 whole wheat flour tortillas

1 tablespoon canola oil, plus more as needed

The rich creaminess of the brie combined with the butternut squash mashed with brown sugar harnesses the flavors of fall.

1. Cook the butternut squash according to the package directions. Transfer to a small bowl and mash with the brown sugar, salt, and pepper.
2. Spread a little brie on each tortilla. Spread the squash mixture on half of each tortilla, then fold the tortillas in half.
3. In a medium nonstick skillet, heat 1 tablespoon oil over medium-high heat until shimmering. Add 1 tortilla, cooking until each side is golden, about 3 minutes per side. Repeat with the remaining tortilla, adding more oil as needed.
4. Remove the quesadillas from the pan and cut each one into 4 wedges.

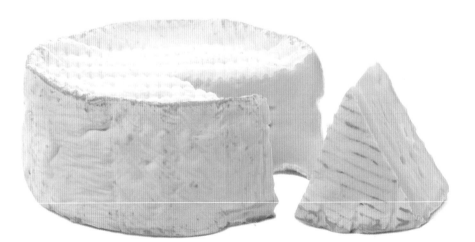

ZUCCHINI *and* POLENTA BAKE

YIELD: 2 servings
PREP TIME: 5 minutes
COOKING TIME: 20 minutes

½ (16-ounce) bag frozen Trader Giotto's Misto alla Griglia

½ (18-ounce) tube Trader Joe's Organic Polenta

1 cup Trader Giotto's Traditional Fresh Ricotta

1½ cups Trader Giotto's Organic Tomato Basil Marinara

Who needs a grill for smoky vegetables when you can open a bag of Trader Giotto's Misto alla Griglia (grilled marinated eggplant and zucchini)?

1. Preheat the oven to 350°F.

2. In a microwave-safe dish, microwave the eggplant and zucchini on high for 2 minutes.

3. Cut the polenta into about 8 (½-inch) slices and arrange them in a baking dish, then add the eggplant and zucchini slices on top.

4. In a small bowl, stir together the ricotta and marinara sauce to combine. Pour over the vegetables and polenta. Bake until hot, about 20 minutes.

RICE *and* BLACK BEANS

YIELD: 2 servings
PREP TIME: 5 minutes
COOKING TIME: 5 minutes

1 (10-ounce) pouch frozen Trader Joe's Brown Rice

1 (15.5-ounce) can Trader Joe's Cuban Style Black Beans

½ (16-ounce) container Trader José's Guacamole Topped with Spicy Pico de Gallo

½ cup sour cream

2 scallions, chopped

Rice and beans are cheap, tasty, and filled with protein.

1. Cook the rice in the microwave according to the package directions.

2. In a large microwave-safe dish, place the cooked rice and stir in the black beans. Microwave on high until hot, 2 to 3 minutes, stirring halfway through.

3. Stir in the guacamole and pico de gallo. Top with dollops of sour cream and scallions.

OLIVE, RED PEPPER, and ARUGULA PIZZA

YIELD: 2 servings
PREP TIME: 10 minutes
COOKING TIME: 16 minutes

flour, as needed

1 ball Trader Joe's Pizza Dough, at room temperature

½ (10-ounce) Trader Joe's Pizza Sauce

1 handful arugula

½ (8-ounce) Trader Joe's Mozzarella, grated

1 red pepper from Trader Joe's Fire-Roasted Red and Yellow Peppers, cut into slices

¼ cup pitted kalamata olives, cut in half

Let your creativity go wild to top this pizza with whatever you have in the fridge. No rolling pin required, just your hands are needed to stretch the dough.

1. Preheat the oven to 450°F.
2. Sprinkle 1 to 2 tablespoons flour onto a cutting board, flouring the cutting board and your hands. Remove the pizza dough from the plastic. Slowly, stretch the dough on the back of your knuckles, rotating the dough and stretching it out into a circular shape. When the dough is stretched out to about 1 foot in diameter, place on the cutting board and stretch the pizza dough even more, using your fingertips.
3. Place the dough directly onto one of the oven racks. Bake until the bottom of the crust is cooked through, about 4 minutes. Using tongs, remove from the oven, and place on the cutting board with the bottom face-up.
4. Spread the pizza sauce onto the dough and top with mozzarella slices. Add the red pepper slices and olives on top of the cheese.
5. Place the pizza in the oven, directly on the wire rack. Bake until the crust is fully cooked and crisp and the cheese has melted, about 12 minutes longer. Using tongs, carefully remove the pizza from the oven.
6. Spread the arugula on top and cut into pieces.

VEGETABLE FRIED RICE

YIELD: 2 servings
PREP TIME: 5 minutes
COOKING TIME: 10 minutes

2 large eggs

1 tablespoon water

1 tablespoon plus 1 teaspoon canola oil, divided

1 (12-ounce) bag sugar snap peas

½ (16-ounce) bag frozen Trader Joe-San's Vegetable Fried Rice, thawed

½ (7-ounce) package Trader Joe's Organic Baked Tofu Savory Flavor, cubed

2 scallions, chopped

The key to good vegetable fried rice is to make sure the frozen rice is fully thawed so each rice grain can get coated with oil and "fried" during the cooking process.

1. Crack the eggs into a small bowl. Add the water and use a fork or whisk to combine.
2. In a medium nonstick skillet, heat 1 teaspoon oil over medium-high heat until shimmering. Add the eggs and use a spatula to constantly move the eggs from the side of the skillet into the center until they're fully cooked, 2 to 3 minutes. Transfer the eggs to a clean bowl and set aside.
3. Microwave the sugar snap peas in their bag on high for 2 minutes.
4. Wipe the skillet clean, then heat the remaining 1 tablespoon oil over high heat until shimmering. Add the vegetable fried rice. Cook until hot, 2 to 3 minutes, stirring constantly. Add the sugar snap peas along with the tofu. Stir to combine and cook until hot, 1 to 2 minutes.
5. Stir in the reserved scrambled eggs and remove from the heat. Sprinkle with scallions.

CHAPTER 7

MICROWAVE MAIN MEALS

These recipes prove that even if you're equipped with just a microwave and a tiny fridge in your dorm, you can still cook tasty meals. Armed with Trader Joe's ingredients and these recipes, there's no excuse not to whip up a feast. Also, Trader Joe's frozen goods are of such high quality they don't have that frozen food taste that others suffer from. No one will ever be the wiser that the entire meal was made in the microwave.

TAMALE-ENCHILADA CASSEROLE

YIELD: 2 servings
PREP TIME: 2 minutes
COOKING TIME: 10 minutes

1 (10-ounce) package Trader José's Handcrafted Chicken and Cheese Tamales

1 (10-ounce) package Trader José's Handcrafted Cheese and Green Chile Tamales

½ (12-ounce) bottle Trader Joe's Enchilada Sauce

1 cup shredded cheese, like Trader Joe's Fancy Shredded Lite Mexican Blend

Pairing tamales with cheese and enchilada sauce creates a delicious treat.

1. Remove the plastic from the tamales and microwave on high until warm, 2 to 3 minutes. Carefully remove the tamales from the corn husks.
2. In a long microwave-safe dish, arrange the tamales in a row. Cut each one in half for quicker heating. Pour the enchilada sauce over the tamales and top with the cheese.
3. Microwave the casserole on high until hot, 3 to 4 more minutes.

BLACK PEPPER SHRIMP *with* FRIED RICE

YIELD: 2 servings
PREP TIME: 1 minute
COOKING TIME: 10 minutes

½ (16-ounce) bag Trader Joe-San's Vegetable Fried Rice

½ (16-ounce) bag Trader Joe's Jumbo Cooked Shrimp (to use raw shrimp, see page 154)

1 tablespoon Trader Joe's Black Pepper Sauce

Be warned—Trader Joe's Black Pepper Sauce packs quite a spicy punch. Use with caution.

1. In a microwave-safe dish, microwave the fried rice on high until hot, 2 to 3 minutes.
2. In another microwave-safe dish, stir together the shrimp and black pepper sauce. Microwave on high until just warm, about 30 seconds. Top the fried rice with the black pepper shrimp.

VEGGIE RISOTTO *with* SHRIMP

YIELD: 2 servings
PREP TIME: 5 minutes
COOKING TIME: 5 minutes

⅓ (16-ounce) bag frozen Trader Joe's Bean so Green

1 (16-ounce) package frozen Trader Joe's Asparagus Risotto

⅓ (16-ounce) bag Trader Joe's Jumbo Cooked Shrimp (to use raw shrimp, see page 154)

2 tablespoons Trader Joe's Grated Parmigiano-Reggiano cheese (optional)

Making risotto, normally a very time-consuming process, has already been tackled thanks to Trader Joe's.

1. Cut the green beans from the vegetable mix into bite-size pieces. Transfer the risotto to a microwave-safe dish and add the vegetable mix on top of it. Microwave on high until hot, 3 to 4 minutes.
2. In another microwave-safe dish, microwave the shrimp until just warm, about 30 seconds.
3. Add the shrimp to the risotto and top with the cheese, if using.

CHICKEN PARMESAN STRIPS

YIELD: 2 servings
PREP TIME: 1 minute
COOKING TIME: 10 minutes

1 (12-ounce) package Trader Joe's Chicken Tenders with Panko Bread Crumbs

1 cup Trader Giotto's Organic Tomato Basil Marinara

2 to 3 slices part-skim mozzarella cheese

2 tablespoons Trader Joe's Grated Parmigiano-Reggiano cheese

A simple take on a comfort food classic.

1. Pierce a few holes in the plastic film over the chicken tenders. Microwave on high until mostly warm, about 2 minutes, then transfer the chicken to a plate. Cover with the marinara sauce and top with the mozzarella and Parmigiano-Reggiano.
2. Microwave on high until hot, 2 to 3 minutes.

PAD THAI

YIELD: 2 servings
PREP TIME: 1 minute
COOKING TIME: 8 minutes

1 frozen Trader Joe's Marinated Chicken Breast Glazed with a Sweet and Tangy Asian Style Marinade

1 (10.5-ounce) package Trader Joe's True Thai Vegetable Pad Thai

½ (16-ounce) package Trader Joe's Harvest Hodgepodge

1 lime, cut into wedges

Trader Joe's Harvest Hodgepodge is a combo of a ton of veggies like baby corn, broccoli, carrots, sugar snap peas, and water chestnuts.

1. In a microwave-safe dish, microwave the chicken on low power until slightly warm, 2 to 3 minutes, then cut the chicken into bite-size pieces.
2. In another microwave-safe dish, add the Pad Thai and Harvest Hodgepodge. Microwave on high for 2 minutes. Add the chicken pieces to the dish and microwave on high until the entire meal is hot, about 1 more minute.

BEEF FAJITAS *with* GUACAMOLE *and* PICO DE GALLO

YIELD: 4 fajitas
PREP TIME: 1 minute
COOKING TIME: 5 minutes

½ (14-ounce) bag frozen Trader Joe's Fire Roasted Bell Pepper and Onions

½ (12-ounce) package frozen Trader Joe's Carne Asada (seasoned beef sirloin)

1½ teaspoons Trader Joe's Taco Seasoning Mix

4 whole wheat flour tortillas

½ (16-ounce) container Trader José's Guacamole topped with Spicy Pico de Gallo

Trader José's Guacamole topped with Spicy Pico de Gallo is a two-for-one deal, offering creamy guacamole and spicy salsa all in one container.

1. In a microwave-safe dish, combine the bell pepper, onions, and carne asada. Microwave on high until hot, about 3 minutes. Sprinkle the taco seasoning on top and stir.

2. Briefly microwave the tortillas until hot, 10 to 15 seconds. Divide the meat and vegetable mixture among the tortillas and top with the guacamole and pico de gallo.

SPAGHETTI MEETS MAC *and* CHEESE

YIELD: 2 servings
PREP TIME: 1 minute
COOKING TIME: 10 minutes

1 (14-ounce) box frozen Joe's Diner Mac 'n Cheese

1 (12-ounce) box frozen Trader Joe's "Just Sauce" Turkey Bolognese

1 teaspoon dried oregano (optional)

By using Trader Joe's ingredients, this delicious meal is accomplished in only 10 minutes.

1. Pierce a few holes in the plastic film over the mac and cheese. Microwave for 5 minutes.

2. Microwave the Bolognese sauce on low power for 2 to 3 minutes. Then microwave on high power until the Bolognese is hot throughout, about 3 minutes.

3. Transfer the hot mac and cheese to a medium bowl. Add the oregano, if using, and stir in about three-quarters of the Bolognese sauce. Reserve the remaining sauce for another use.

CARNE ASADA POLENTA "LASAGNE"

YIELD: 2 servings
PREP TIME: 10 minutes
COOKING TIME: 5 minutes

Instead of using strips of pasta, this dish layers polenta with cheese, mushrooms, and beef.

1½ cups Trader Joe's Traditional Fresh Ricotta

2 tablespoons Trader Joe's Condensed Cream of Portabella Mushroom Soup

½ (12-ounce) package frozen Trader Joe's Carne Asada (seasoned beef sirloin)

2 scallions, chopped

½ (18-ounce) tube Trader Joe's Organic Polenta

1. In a small bowl, stir together the ricotta, soup, carne asada, and scallions.
2. Cut the polenta into rounds about ¼ inch thick. In a medium microwave-safe dish, make one layer of polenta using 5 to 6 slices and top with half of the ricotta mixture.
3. Add another layer of polenta, using the remaining 5 to 6 slices. Top with the remaining ricotta mixture, smoothing it over the polenta slices.
4. Microwave until hot, 5 to 6 minutes.

STUFFED RED PEPPERS *with* CHICKEN *and* ORZO

YIELD: 2 servings
PREP TIME: 5 minutes
COOKING TIME: 5 minutes

This meal is quick and delicious and tastes like it took a long time to assemble, instead of just minutes.

1 (18-ounce) package Trader Joe's Greek Style Chicken with Orzo, Spinach and Feta Cheese

1 (24-ounce) jar Trader Joe's Roasted Red Peppers

¾ cup Trader Joe's Crumbled Feta with Mediterranean Herbs

1. Cut the chicken and olives from the Greek Style Chicken into bite-size pieces. Mix the ingredients together.
2. Lay the peppers in a microwave-safe dish. Using a spoon, fill each pepper with the orzo mixture. Microwave on high until hot, 2 to 3 minutes.
3. Crumble the feta on top of the peppers and microwave again until the cheese is melted, 30 seconds to 1 minute.

PENNE MEATBALLS *with* ARRABIATA SAUCE

YIELD: 2 servings
PREP TIME: 1 minute
COOKING TIME: 10 minutes

½ (16-ounce) bag frozen Trader Joe's "Just Pasta" Penne

½ (16-ounce) package frozen Trader Joe's Flame Broiled Turkey Meatballs Fully Cooked

½ (25-ounce) jar Trader Joe's Arrabiata Sauce

Trader Joe's Grated Parmigiano-Reggiano cheese, as needed (optional)

Arrabiata translates to "angry" in Italian, so this sauce's name comes from the added heat of chile peppers.

1. Microwave the pasta according to the package directions. Set aside.
2. In a medium microwave-safe dish, microwave the meatballs on high for 2 minutes. Then pour the arrabiata sauce into the dish with the meatballs and microwave on high until the sauce and meatballs are heated, 2 to 3 more minutes.
3. Open the bag of pasta and add it to the dish with the sauce and meatballs. Toss to combine and sprinkle with the cheese, if using.

TORTILLA CHILI CHEESE DOGS

YIELD: 4 hot dogs
PREP TIME: 1 minute
COOKING TIME: 10 minutes

⅓ (15-ounce) can Trader Joe's Turkey Chili

¼ (11.5-ounce) jar Trader Joe's Queso Cheese Dip

4 Trader Joe's All Natural Uncured All-Beef Hot Dogs

4 whole wheat flour tortillas

When you're low on time between classes and just want a quick bite to eat, turn to this chili and cheese hot dog goodness.

1. Pour the chili into a bowl and top with the queso dip. Microwave on high, stirring halfway through, until hot, 3 to 4 minutes.
2. Wrap the hot dogs in paper towels and microwave on high until hot, up to 1 minute.
3. Briefly microwave the tortillas until warm, 10 to 15 seconds. Lay the tortillas on a cutting board and add a hot dog to the middle of each one. Spoon the chili-queso mixture over each hot dog until covered.
4. Wrap the tortillas burrito-style, folding up the bottom edge first and then rolling the hot dog in the tortilla so the chili doesn't slip out.

GREEN CHILE SHEPHERD'S PIE

YIELD: 2 servings
PREP TIME: 5 minutes
COOKING TIME: 10 minutes

½ (20-ounce) package Trader Joe's Party Size Mini Meatballs

½ (28-ounce) package frozen Trader Joe's Mashed Potatoes (about 25 medallions)

½ (16-ounce) bag frozen Trader Joe's Roasted Corn

½ (4-ounce) can Trader Joe's New Mexican Hatch Valley Roasted Diced Green Chiles

½ cup Trader Joe's Fancy Shredded Mexican Cheese

Shepherd's pie is one of my favorite meals. For a Southwestern spin, the mashed potatoes are combined with green chiles and melty cheese.

1. Cut the meatballs in half and arrange them in a microwave-safe dish. Microwave according to the package directions.
2. In two separate dishes, microwave the potatoes and the corn on high until warm, just 2 to 3 minutes. Layer the corn on top of the meatballs.
3. Mix the chiles into the mashed potatoes, then layer them on top of the corn. Top with a layer of cheese and microwave on high until hot, 2 to 3 minutes.

CHAPTER 8

SIMPLE SIDES

Give vegetables a chance. You know you want to. And, trust me on this, don't judge veggies by the wilted, soggy ones they serve at the cafeteria. Trader Joe's superfresh vegetables are usually prewashed, prechopped, and, in a lot of cases, can be cooked in the plastic pouch you buy them in.

There's no reason not to add these babies into your diet in a way that's tasty. In these recipes, broccoli is tossed with olive oil and dried cherries, corn on the cob is slathered with cheese, and carrots are glazed with honey. Also, check out Rice and Vermicelli and Pesto-Roasted Potatoes—both potatoes and rice are cheap ways to get creative with side dishes.

If you're overwhelmed at the thought of cooking a side dish at the same time as a main dish to serve it with, don't fret. These recipes are simple to put together and don't require much multitasking.

HEARTS *of* PALM *with* MANGO *and* ONION

YIELD: 2 servings
PREP TIME: 10 minutes

1 (14.5-ounce) package Trader
Joe's Hearts of Palm, drained
and rinsed

1 mango

¼ cup diced red onion
(see page 153)

2 teaspoons olive oil

kosher salt and freshly ground
black pepper

Hearts of palm are exactly what they sound like—a vegetable harvested from the inner core of a certain type of palm tree.

1. Cut each heart of palm into 1-inch pieces. Place in a small bowl. Dice the mango and add it to the bowl, along with the red onion and olive oil. Season to taste with salt and pepper.
2. Using a spoon, mix all the ingredients together to combine.

ROASTED TOMATOES

YIELD: 2 servings
PREP TIME: 5 minutes
COOKING TIME: 30 minutes

2 (16-ounce) containers cherry
tomatoes

1 tablespoon olive oil

½ teaspoon kosher salt

¼ teaspoon freshly ground black
pepper

This vegan recipe for roasted cherry tomatoes is amazingly easy. All you do is season and shove in the oven to let it work its roasting magic.

1. Preheat the oven to 400°F. Line a rimmed baking sheet with foil.
2. Spread the tomatoes on the prepared baking sheet. Drizzle with the olive oil and sprinkle with the salt and pepper. Toss the tomatoes to coat in the oil and seasonings.
3. Bake the tomatoes until crinkly and roasted, 25 to 30 minutes, stirring just once halfway through the cooking time.

ASPARAGUS *with* AIOLI

YIELD: 2 servings
PREP TIME: 5 minutes
COOKING TIME: 2 minutes

kosher salt and freshly ground
black pepper

1 (12-ounce) package asparagus

squeeze of lemon

2 tablespoons Trader Joe's Aioli
Garlic Mustard Sauce

Asparagus doesn't require much enhancement, but dipping it into a flavorful aioli adds a little excitement.

1. Bring a medium pot three-quarters full of salted water to a boil over high heat.
2. To trim the asparagus, bend the bottom part of the asparagus, 1 to 2 inches from the bottom, and the stalk will snap at the point where tender meets tough. Add the asparagus and cook briefly until tender, just 1 to 2 minutes. Transfer the asparagus to a plate.
3. Sprinkle the asparagus with salt, pepper, and a squeeze of lemon juice. Serve with the aioli as a dipping sauce.

PARMESAN *and* BREAD CRUMB-CRUSTED TOMATOES

YIELD: 2 servings
PREP TIME: 5 minutes
COOKING TIME: 10 minutes

2 medium tomatoes

2 tablespoons Trader Joe's Japanese-Style Panko Bread Crumbs

1½ tablespoons Trader Joe's Grated Parmigiano-Reggiano cheese, plus extra for topping

2 tablespoons olive oil

¼ teaspoon kosher salt

I have yet to serve these tomatoes to anyone who doesn't immediately devour them and ask for the recipe.

1. Preheat the oven to 400°F. Line a rimmed baking sheet with foil.
2. Cut the tomatoes into ½-inch slices, 4 or 5 slices per tomato. Transfer the slices to the prepared baking sheet.
3. In a small bowl, combine the bread crumbs, cheese, olive oil, and salt. Divide the mixture among the tomato slices, mounding it on top of each one. Sprinkle with additional cheese.
4. Bake until the tomatoes are soft and the crust is crispy, 8 to 10 minutes.

BEETS *with* MINT GREMOLATA

YIELD: 2 servings
PREP TIME: 10 minutes

1 teaspoon grated lemon zest

¼ teaspoon Trader Joe's Crushed Garlic

2 tablespoons chopped mint

juice of ½ lemon

1 tablespoon olive oil

kosher salt and freshly ground black pepper

1 (8-ounce) package Trader Joe's Steamed and Peeled Baby Beets

I've converted many beet haters with this sweet, earthy vegan recipe.

1. To make the gremolata, in a medium bowl, combine the lemon zest, garlic, mint, lemon juice, and olive oil. Season to taste with salt and pepper.
2. On a plate, use a butter knife to carefully cut the beets into bite-size pieces. Add the beets to the bowl with the gremolata, stirring to combine.

SUGAR SNAP PEAS *with* BOK CHOY

YIELD: 2 servings
PREP TIME: 5 minutes
COOKING TIME: 10 minutes

1 (3-ounce) package
baby bok choy

1 (12-ounce) package
sugar snap peas

1 teaspoon canola oil

2 tablespoons Trader Joe's
Island Soyaki

kosher salt and freshly ground
black pepper

Trader Joe's island-inspired spin on teriyaki sauce gives the baby bok choy and sugar snap peas a bright, sweet boost.

1. Cut off the stems of the baby bok choy. Cut the bok choy into pieces, making the leaves larger and the stems smaller so it all cooks evenly.
2. Microwave the sugar snap peas in their bag on high for 2 minutes.
3. Meanwhile, heat the oil in a medium skillet over medium-high heat until shimmering. Add the baby bok choy to the pan and cook, stirring constantly, until the leaves are just wilted, about 1 minute. Add the Soyaki sauce to the pan, stirring constantly. Add the peas, sautéing and stirring to coat.
4. Test a bok choy stem for tenderness and remove the pan from the heat. Season to taste with salt and pepper.

BROCCOLI *with* DRIED CHERRIES

YIELD: 2 servings
PREP TIME: 10 minutes
COOKING TIME: 10 minutes

kosher salt and freshly ground
black pepper

2 heads broccoli

¼ cup olive oil

1 tablespoon Trader Joe's
Crushed Garlic

½ teaspoon red chile pepper
flakes

2 tablespoons lemon juice

½ cup dried cherries

This vegan side is great with a vegetarian main dish or seafood, and it can also be paired with a fattier beef dish if you're looking to balance out the meal.

1. Bring a medium pot three-quarters full of salted water to a boil over high heat.
2. Cut the broccoli into even bite-size pieces. When the water is boiling, add the broccoli and cook until fork-tender, about 5 minutes. Drain into a colander and reserve.
3. In the pot, heat the oil over medium-high heat until shimmering. Add the garlic and chile pepper flakes and cook, stirring constantly, for 1 minute. Remove from the heat and add the lemon juice and dried cherries. Add the cooked broccoli, stirring to combine. Season to taste with salt and pepper.

MEXICAN CORN *on the* COB

YIELD: 4 pieces corn on the cob
PREP TIME: 5 minutes
COOKING TIME: 5 minutes

1 (4-pack) Trader Joe's Corn on
the Cob

2 tablespoons mayonnaise

1 tablespoon Trader Joe's Taco
Seasoning Mix

1 tablespoon Trader Joe's Grated
Parmigiano-Reggiano cheese

This is practically the only way I eat my corn on the cob these days.

1. If your pot is narrower than your ears of corn, cut them in half. Bring a medium pot three-quarters full of salted water to a boil over high heat. Add the corn, covering it with water. Cook until the kernels are bright yellow and tender, 3 to 4 minutes. Transfer the corn to a plate.
2. Using a butter knife, slather the corn with mayonnaise. Sprinkle with taco seasoning and cheese.

STUFFED PEAR HALVES

YIELD: 2 servings
PREP TIME: 10 minutes
COOKING TIME: 15 minutes

1 (25-ounce) jar Trader Joe's Pear Halves in White Grape Juice (5 pear halves)

1 tablespoon cream cheese, softened in the microwave for 10 seconds

2 tablespoons Trader Joe's Crumbled Blue Cheese

6 Trader Joe's Triple Ginger Snaps

Sometimes I serve these pears on a bed of arugula for an easy, delicious salad.

1. Preheat the oven to 400°F. Line a rimmed baking sheet with foil.
2. Arrange the pear halves on the prepared baking sheet.
3. In a small bowl, mix the cream cheese and blue cheese together. Mound a dollop of the mixture into each pear half.
4. Seal the ginger snaps into a plastic bag and pound into crumbs with a rolling pin or the bottom of a pan. Pour the crumbs over the pears. Bake until warm, about 15 minutes.

PESTO-ROASTED POTATOES

YIELD: 2 servings
PREP TIME: 5 minutes
COOKING TIME: 65 minutes

1 (16-ounce) bag fingerling potatoes

1 tablespoon plus 2 teaspoons olive oil, divided

½ teaspoon kosher salt

¼ teaspoon freshly ground black pepper

2 tablespoons Trader Giotto's Genova Pesto

Pesto adds a flare of flavor to these roasted potatoes without much extra work.

1. Preheat the oven to 400°F. Line a rimmed baking sheet with foil.
2. Cut each potato in half lengthwise. Spread the potatoes on the prepared baking sheet. Drizzle with 1 tablespoon oil and sprinkle with the salt and pepper. Toss the potatoes to coat and arrange in a single layer. Bake until fork-tender, about 1 hour, stirring once halfway through.
3. In a small bowl, place the pesto and thin it with the remaining 2 teaspoons oil.
4. Remove the potatoes from the oven. Drizzle the pesto sauce over the potatoes, stirring with a spatula. Return the potatoes to the oven for 5 minutes.

BAKED SWEET POTATO SPEARS
with MEXICAN SPICES

YIELD: 2 servings
PREP TIME: 5 minutes
COOKING TIME: 30 to 40 minutes

2 (12-ounce) bags Trader Joe's Sweet Potato Spears

1½ tablespoons olive oil

1 tablespoon Trader Joe's Taco Seasoning Mix

½ teaspoon kosher salt

These presliced sweet potato spears are a great item—no washing or slicing required.

1. Preheat the oven to 400°F. Line a rimmed baking sheet with foil.
2. Spread the sweet potato spears on the prepared baking sheet. Drizzle with the oil and sprinkle with the taco seasoning and salt. Toss the sweet potato spears to coat and arrange in a single layer.
3. Bake until tender, 30 to 40 minutes, stirring once halfway through.

GREEN CHILE CORNBREAD MUFFINS

YIELD: 12 muffins
PREP TIME: 10 minutes
COOKING TIME: 25 minutes

1 egg

½ cup canola oil

¾ cup milk

1 (15-ounce) box Trader Joe's Cornbread Mix

¾ cup frozen Trader Joe's Roasted Corn, thawed

1 (4-ounce) can Trader Joe's New Mexico Hatch Valley Fire Roasted Diced Green Chiles

unsalted butter

Enjoy these vegan muffins with a hearty dinner entrée, and then snack on a leftover muffin on the way to class.

1. Preheat the oven to 350°F. Spray 12 muffin cups with cooking spray.
2. In a large bowl, whisk together the egg, oil, and milk. Stir in the cornbread mix, using a spoon or spatula to combine. Stir in the corn and chiles.
3. Fill each prepared muffin cup three-quarters full with batter.
4. Bake until a toothpick or knife inserted in the center of a muffin comes out clean, 20 to 25 minutes. Remove the muffins from the oven and let cool 15 to 20 minutes. Serve with butter.

Note: If you don't have a muffin tin, just bake the cornbread in an 8 x 8 x 2-inch pan and increase the baking time to 35 to 40 minutes.

GLAZED CARROTS

YIELD: 2 servings
PREP TIME: 10 minutes
COOKING TIME: 30 minutes

Roasting gives root vegetables like carrots a nice sweetness; honey enhances it even more.

1 (16-ounce) bag Trader Joe's Organics Cut and Peeled Carrots

1 tablespoon olive oil

kosher salt and freshly ground black pepper

½ orange

1 tablespoon honey

1. Preheat the oven to 400°F. Line a rimmed baking sheet with foil.
2. Spread the carrots on the prepared baking sheet. Drizzle with the oil and sprinkle with salt and pepper. Squeeze the orange half over the carrots. Toss the carrots to coat, then arrange in a single layer.
3. Bake until the carrots are fork-tender, about 30 minutes, stirring halfway through. Remove from the oven, and increase the temperature to 425°F. Drizzle the honey over the carrots and return them to the oven to let the honey caramelize, about 5 minutes.

RICE *and* VERMICELLI

YIELD: 2 servings
PREP TIME: 5 minutes
COOKING TIME: 25 minutes

Browning and cooking the vermicelli noodles adds a nuttiness to the dish.

1 tablespoon canola oil

⅓ cup chopped Trader Joe's Vermicelli Noodles

½ cup long-grain white rice

1 cup chicken broth, or 1 cup water and 1 (9.6-gram) pouch Trader Joe's Savory Chicken Concentrate

1 tablespoon unsalted butter

kosher salt and freshly ground black pepper

1. In a medium pot, heat the oil over medium-high heat until shimmering. Add the noodles, stirring to coat. Cook, stirring constantly, until the noodles have browned, then add the rice and chicken broth.
2. Let the liquid come to a boil, then reduce the heat to low. Cover and let simmer until rice is tender, about 20 minutes. Remove from the heat and let sit for 10 minutes.
3. Add the butter to the rice and stir. Season to taste with salt and pepper.

CURRIED COUSCOUS *with* APPLES

YIELD: 2 servings
PREP TIME: 5 minutes
COOKING TIME: 12 minutes

1 tablespoon unsalted butter

¾ cup Trader Joe's
Israeli Couscous

2 teaspoons curry powder

1 red apple,
cut into bite-size pieces

1 cup water or chicken broth

kosher salt and freshly ground
black pepper

The crunch of apple and spice of curry make this dish shine.

1. In a small pot over medium-high heat, place the butter, couscous, and curry powder, stirring to coat the couscous with the butter and curry powder. Add the apple and water or chicken broth, stirring to combine. Bring the liquid to a boil, then cover the pot. Reduce the heat to low and cook until the couscous is tender, 10 to 12 minutes.
2. Remove from the heat and season with salt and pepper.

CHAPTER 9

QUICK & HEARTY BRAIN FOOD FOR FINALS

When you're struggling to cram for finals—not to mention finish that ten-page paper that's due tomorrow—you need every bit of brain power you can get to help focus your thoughts. And guess what? There are certain foods that nature has filled with nutrients and vitamins that work to help you concentrate throughout the day. From nuts to lentils to berries, some ingredients have been proven to strengthen mental power. Use these recipes to feed both your stomach and your mind during a hectic week of tests.

TROPICAL SMOOTHIE

YIELD: 2 servings
PREP TIME: 5 minutes

1 cup low-fat plain yogurt

½ cup orange juice

1½ cups frozen mango chunks

1 teaspoon honey (optional)

Smoothies are a quick and sustaining way to get food into your system during a chaotic week.

1. In a blender, place the yogurt, orange juice, mango chunks, and honey, if using.
2. Purée until the mango chunks disappear and the smoothie is thoroughly blended, 30 seconds to 1 minute.

VERY BERRY SMOOTHIE

YIELD: 2 servings
PREP TIME: 5 minutes

1½ cups Trader Joe's Lowfat Kefir Strawberry Cultured Milk or Pomegranate Cultured Milk

1 banana, coarsely chopped

½ (16-ounce) bag frozen Trader Joe's Very Cherry Berry Blend

When you're stressed and need to focus on cramming for tomorrow's test, berries are essential for your diet because scientists have determined that they lead to a clearer mind.

1. In a blender, place the cultured milk, banana, and berries.
2. Purée until the smoothie is thoroughly blended, 30 seconds to 1 minute.

OATMEAL *with* BERRIES *and* ALMONDS

YIELD: 1 to 2 servings
PREP TIME: 1 minute
COOKING TIME: 3 minutes

The vitamins and nutrients in Trader Joe's Oatmeal Complete, combined with the brain-boosting ability of blueberries and the staying power of almonds, make this a rockin' meal to start a test day on the right foot.

2 (40-gram) packets Trader Joe's Oatmeal Complete

1¼ cups water

¼ cup frozen blueberries

½ cup milk

¼ cup sliced almonds

1. Empty the oatmeal packets into a medium microwave-safe bowl. Stir in the water and frozen blueberries.
2. Microwave on high until hot, 2 to 3 minutes, stirring once halfway through.
3. Stir in the milk and top with the almonds.

MICROWAVE SCRAMBLED EGGS *with* SMOKED SALMON

YIELD: 2 servings
PREP TIME: 5 minutes
COOKING TIME: 2 to 3 minutes

Eggs are one of the most cost-effective ways of getting a large dose of protein into your diet, which can provide a boost of energy throughout the day.

3 large eggs

¼ teaspoon kosher salt

¼ teaspoon freshly ground black pepper

1 tablespoon water

1 tablespoon cream cheese

½ (4-ounce) package Trader Joe's Wild Smoked Sockeye Salmon, coarsely chopped

chopped chives, for garnish

1. In a medium microwave-safe dish, crack the eggs and add the salt, pepper, and water. Lightly beat the eggs with a whisk or fork to combine.
2. Microwave the eggs on high for 30 seconds. Using a spoon, combine the cooked eggs on the edge of the dish with the uncooked eggs in the middle. Microwave for 30 seconds longer. Stir again.
3. Repeat Step 2 until the scrambled eggs are fluffy and cooked, being careful not to overcook them. The total cooking time will depend on the power strength of the microwave but should be 2 to 3 minutes.
4. Remove the scrambled eggs from the microwave and stir in the cream cheese and smoked salmon. Top with the chives.

AVOCADO TOAST

YIELD: 2 pieces
PREP TIME: 5 minutes
COOKING TIME: 1 minute

2 slices Trader Joe's Soft 10
Grain Bread

½ cup Trader Joe's Traditional
Fresh Ricotta

1 avocado, diced
(for dicing tips, see page 152)

juice of ½ lemon

½ teaspoon kosher salt

Avocado contains monounsaturated fat (the good kind of fat), which goes hand-in-hand with better brain activity.

1. Toast the bread in a toaster.
2. Meanwhile, in a small bowl, mash together the ricotta, avocado, lemon juice, and salt with a fork to combine.
3. Spread the avocado mixture onto each piece of toast.

TRAIL MIX *with* CHOCOLATE-COVERED EDAMAME

YIELD: 2 servings
PREP TIME: 5 minutes

1 cup Trader Joe's Roasted and
Salted Mixed Nuts with Peanuts

1 cup Trader Joe's Dark
Chocolate Edamame

1 cup dried mixed tropical fruit

It's the caffeine and sugar from dark chocolate that can give you a slight boost of energy to improve brain power.

1. In a small bowl, combine the nuts, edamame, and dried fruit.
2. Transfer the trail mix to a sealable plastic bag for easier portability.

POTATO FRITTATA

YIELD: 2 to 3 servings
PREP TIME: 5 minutes
COOKING TIME: 10 minutes

4 hashbrowns from frozen
Trader Joe's Hashbrowns

1 tablespoon canola oil

3 large eggs

½ teaspoon kosher salt

¼ teaspoon freshly ground black
pepper

½ cup Trader Joe's Shredded
Pepper Jack Cheese Blend

A frittata is akin to an omelet, except the ingredients are mixed with the eggs instead of folded inside of them—and it's a heck of a lot easier to make.

1. Preheat the oven to 400°F.

2. Toast the hash browns in a toaster to defrost. Chop the hash browns into medium dice.

3. In an oven-safe nonstick skillet, heat the oil over medium-high heat until shimmering. Add the hash browns in a single layer, frying until slightly crisp on each side, 6 to 7 minutes total.

4. Meanwhile, in a medium bowl, place the eggs, salt, and pepper. Mix together with a fork or a whisk.

5. Pour the eggs on top of the hash browns, gently stirring with a spatula until the egg mixture has set on the bottom, 1 to 2 minutes.

6. Transfer the pan to the oven and bake until the top of the frittata is almost set and puffy. Sprinkle with the cheese and continue to bake until the cheese melts, 1 to 2 minutes more.

HARVEST GRAINS BLEND *with* SPINACH

YIELD: 2 servings
PREP TIME: 5 minutes
COOKING TIME: 15 minutes

1 tablespoon olive oil

1 (6-ounce) bag baby spinach

1¼ cups Trader Joe's Harvest Grains Blend

1¾ cups vegetable or chicken broth

½ teaspoon kosher salt, or more

¼ teaspoon freshly ground black pepper, or more

Greens, like spinach, are a superstar source of folate and vitamin B, which lead to better memory recall. Trader Joe's Harvest Grains Blend is a hearty, tasty mix of Israeli couscous, baby chickpeas, orzo, and red quinoa that will keep you full and focused during a cram session.

1. In a medium pot, heat the oil over medium-high heat until shimmering.
2. Add half the spinach, stirring until wilted, about 1 minute. Add the remaining spinach, stirring until wilted, about 1 minute longer.
3. Add the grains, stirring to coat with the oil. Pour in the vegetable or chicken broth, stirring to combine with the grains. Add the salt and pepper, stir, and bring to a boil.
4. Reduce the heat to low. Cover the pot and let simmer until all of the liquid has been absorbed, 12 to 15 minutes. Taste and adjust the seasonings with salt and pepper, as needed.

SALMON BURGERS *with* TZATZIKI

YIELD: 2 sandwiches
PREP TIME: 1 minute
COOKING TIME: 8 minutes

2 teaspoons canola oil

2 Trader Joe's Premium Salmon Patties

2 Trader Joe's Honey Wheat Hamburger Buns

2 tablespoons Trader Joe's Tzatziki (creamy garlic cucumber dip)

Salmon is rich in DHA, an omega-3 fatty acid that's full of brain-boosting power, which improves your attention span in times of marathon studying or test taking.

1. In a nonstick skillet, heat the oil over medium-high heat until shimmering.
2. Add the salmon patties and cook until done, 3 to 4 minutes per side. Pierce one of the patties with a small knife to see whether it's cooked to your liking.
3. Meanwhile, warm the buns in the microwave.
4. Place the salmon patties on the hamburger bun bottoms. Top generously with the tzatziki and add the bun tops.

WARMED CHICKEN SALAD *with* GREEN TEA

YIELD: 2 servings
PREP TIME: 5 minutes
COOKING TIME: 5 minutes

1 Marinated Chicken Breast Glazed with a Sweet and Tangy Asian Style Marinade

½ cup Trader Joe's Shelled Soybeans, Ready to Eat

1 tablespoon mayonnaise

¼ teaspoon kosher salt

¼ teaspoon freshly ground black pepper

1 scallion, chopped

1 tea bag Trader Joe's Green Tea

Edamame is a powerful protein source to help you get through a mammoth week of work, and green tea is a rock star for the brain.

1. Heat the chicken breast according to the package directions, then cut the chicken into bite-size pieces.
2. In a medium bowl, place the soybeans, mayonnaise, salt, pepper, and scallion. Open the tea bag, measure 1 teaspoon green tea leaves, and add it to the mixture. Discard the remainder of the tea bag.
3. Stir the mayonnaise mixture together, then add the chicken chunks and stir to combine.

ROASTED CHICKEN *with* LEEKS *and* APPLES

YIELD: 2 servings
PREP TIME: 10 minutes
COOKING TIME: 35 minutes

1 tablespoon canola oil

4 pieces Trader Joe's Organic Free Range Chicken Boneless Thighs

½ teaspoon kosher salt, or more

¼ teaspoon freshly ground black pepper, or more

1 (6-ounce) package Trader Joe's Trimmed Leeks, cut in half lengthwise, then crosswise into 1-inch pieces

½ (16-ounce) bag Trader Joe's Sliced Apples

1 tablespoon unsalted butter, cut into small pieces

Apples are known to improve cognitive function—as if you need an excuse to add more apples to your diet.

1. Preheat the oven to 400°F.
2. In a medium oven-safe skillet, heat the oil over medium-high heat until shimmering.
3. Season the chicken thighs with salt and pepper. Add the chicken to the oil and cook just 2 to 3 minutes, letting the bottom sides of the chicken brown.
4. Remove the chicken from the skillet. Add the leeks and apples to the skillet and place the chicken pieces on top. Scatter the butter over and transfer the skillet to the oven. Bake for 30 minutes, stirring once halfway through. Cut into the thickest chicken piece to determine that it's no longer pink. Adjust the seasoning with salt and pepper, as needed.

LENTILS *with* CHICKEN SAUSAGE

YIELD: 2 servings
PREP TIME: 5 minutes
COOKING TIME: 10 minutes

1 (12-ounce) package frozen Trader Joe's Curried Lentils on Cumin Flavored Basmati Rice

2 teaspoons canola oil

½ (14-ounce) package Trader Joe's Mango Chicken Sausage (2½ sausages)

juice of ½ lime

Lentils will give you a good supply of glucose, which powers the body with sustained energy through the day.

1. Pierce a few holes in the plastic over the curried lentils and rice and microwave on high until hot, 3 to 4 minutes.
2. Cut the sausage into bite-size slices.
3. In a medium skillet, heat the oil over medium-high heat until shimmering. Add the sausage and cook until browned, 3 to 5 minutes.
4. Transfer the lentils and rice to a large bowl. Add the lime juice, stirring to combine, then add the sausage.

CHAPTER 10

SPECIAL OCCASIONS

Let's face facts: You're busy in college and don't want to devote a ton of time to cooking. That's why most of the recipes in this book lean toward the quick-and-easy side of things.

But sometimes, just sometimes, you want to cook a little something special.

Maybe you've worked hard all week through a slew of tests and deserve a special Saturday dinner. Or you're hosting your first dinner party, having a romantic date, or just want something a little fancy.

These recipes deliver on your occasional need to take dinner to the next level. Don't worry—they're still on the easy side. But they'll taste like you've been slaving for hours.

EGGPLANT PARMESAN LASAGNE

YIELD: 4 servings
PREP TIME: 15 minutes
COOKING TIME: 65 minutes

1 (15-ounce) container Trader Giotto's Traditional Fresh Ricotta

1 large egg

1 cup Trader Joe's Grated Parmigiano-Reggiano cheese, or more (optional)

1 (16-ounce) box frozen Trader Joe's Eggplant Cutlets

1 (25-ounce) jar Trader Giotto's Organic Tomato Basil Marinara

8 Trader Joe's Italian Lasagna Noodles No Boiling—Oven Ready

Take a few Trader Joe's ingredients, mix them together, and voilà—you have an impressive dinner either to serve when guests come over or to take to a potluck.

1. Preheat the oven to 375°F.
2. In a medium bowl, stir together the ricotta, egg, and Parmigiano-Reggiano, if using.
3. In a small baking dish, start assembling the lasagne: Arrange 4 to 5 eggplant cutlets in the bottom. Top with one-third of the tomato sauce and 2 lasagna noodles.
4. Next, layer one-half of the ricotta mixture and 2 more lasagna noodles on top. Arrange a second layer of 4 to 5 eggplant cutlets in the dish, then one-third of the tomato sauce and 2 more lasagna noodles.
5. Add the remaining one-half of the ricotta mixture and top with the remaining 2 lasagna noodles.
6. Pour the remaining one-third of the tomato sauce over the lasagne. Cover the dish with foil. Bake until the noodles are fully cooked, 60 to 65 minutes. Remove from the oven and top with extra Parmigiano-Reggiano cheese, if desired.

CRAB CAKES BENEDICT

YIELD: 4 servings
PREP TIME: 5 minutes
COOKING TIME: 10 minutes

This is a fancy brunch meal for when the occasion arises.

4 teaspoons olive oil, divided

1 (6-ounce) bag baby spinach

1 teaspoon Trader Joe's Crushed Garlic

2 (6-ounce) packages Trader Joe's Maryland Style Crab Cakes

2 whole grain English muffins

2 to 3 tablespoons Trader Joe's Hollandaise Sauce

chopped chives, for garnish

1. In a nonstick skillet, heat 2 teaspoons oil over high heat until shimmering. Add one-half of the spinach, stirring until wilted, about 1 minute. Add the garlic and the remaining spinach, stirring until all the spinach is wilted and the garlic is golden, about 1 minute longer. Transfer the spinach to a bowl and set aside.

2. Wipe the pan clean with a paper towel. Heat the remaining 2 teaspoons oil over medium-high heat until shimmering. Add the frozen crab cakes to the pan and cook until hot, about 2 minutes per side. Split the muffins and toast.

3. Place a muffin half on each plate. Pile each one with one-fourth of the reserved spinach and top with a crab cake.

4. In a microwave-safe dish, microwave the hollandaise sauce on high until warm, about 1 minute. Drizzle the sauce over the crab cakes and garnish with the chives.

SALMON *with* MIREPOIX

YIELD: 4 servings
PREP TIME: 10 minutes
COOKING TIME: 15 minutes

1 tablespoon canola oil

1 (14.5-ounce) container Trader Joe's Mirepoix (onion, celery, and carrots)

3 tablespoons carrot juice

1 frozen Trader Joe's Wild Alaskan Sockeye Salmon Fillet (about 1 pound), thawed

½ teaspoon kosher salt

¼ teaspoon freshly ground black pepper

juice of ½ lemon

This is based on a Julia Child recipe in which salmon is cooked on a bed of onion, celery, and carrots with white wine.

1. Preheat the oven to 350°F.
2. In a large oven-safe skillet, heat the oil over medium-high heat until shimmering.
3. Add the mirepoix to the pan and cook, stirring occasionally, until the onion is soft, about 5 minutes. Remove the skillet from the heat. Add the carrot juice and stir to combine.
4. Season the salmon with salt and pepper, and place it on top of the vegetable mixture. Cover the pan with foil.
5. Bake for 12 to 15 minutes, depending on the size and thickness of the salmon fillet. Pierce the salmon with a small knife to see whether it's cooked to your liking. Remove from the oven and drizzle with lemon juice.

LEMON PASTA *with* CLAMS *and* CHIVES

YIELD: 4 servings
PREP TIME: 10 minutes
COOKING TIME: 10 minutes

This is a luxurious, indulgent pasta that will impress any guest.

2 (8-ounce) packages Trader Joe's Lemon Pepper Pappardelle Pasta

1 tablespoon olive oil

1 (16-ounce) package frozen Trader Joe's Steamer Clams in Garlic Butter Sauce

1 (17.5-ounce) jar Trader Giotto's White Clam Sauce

2 tablespoons chopped chives

1. Bring a medium pot of salted water to a boil over high heat. Cook the pappardelle until al dente (see page 153), about 8 minutes. Drain and toss with the olive oil.
2. Pierce a few holes in the plastic film over the clams. Microwave on high for 5 minutes. Shake the container to coat the clams with the sauce. Let sit for 2 minutes to steam.
3. In a medium skillet, heat the clam sauce over medium-high heat until hot, 2 to 3 minutes. Add the pasta to the sauce and toss to coat.
4. Remove the skillet from the heat and add the clams with a few tablespoons of the garlic butter sauce. Garnish with the chives.

LOBSTER SAUCE *with* LANGOUSTINE

YIELD: 4 servings
PREP TIME: 5 minutes
COOKING TIME: 15 minutes

¾ (16-ounce) package Trader Giotto's Organic Spaghetti

1 tablespoon olive oil

1 (12-ounce) container Trader Joe's Lobster Bisque

1 (12-ounce) bag frozen Trader Joe's Langoustine Tails, defrosted and drained

2 tablespoons minced parsley (optional)

This is the dish to make for a romantic Valentine's Day dinner, Trader Joe's–style.

1. Cook the spaghetti according to the package directions. Reserve ¾ cup pasta water, then drain the pasta and toss with the olive oil.
2. In a large skillet, add the lobster bisque and reserved pasta water and heat over medium heat, 4 to 5 minutes.
3. Add the langoustines to the pan and cook until warm, just 1 or 2 minutes. (The langoustines are already fully cooked, so you don't want to overcook them.)
4. Remove from the heat and add the pasta, using a fork or tongs to coat. Top with parsley, if using.

Note: Langoustines are small, pink crustaceans that look similar to crawfish with a taste more akin to lobster.

ISRAELI COUSCOUS *with* LEMON SHRIMP

YIELD: 4 servings
PREP TIME: 5 minutes
COOKING TIME: 12 minutes

2½ tablespoons unsalted butter, divided

1½ cups Israeli couscous

2 cups water

kosher salt and freshly ground black pepper

juice of 2 lemons

½ cup olive oil

½ cup Trader Joe's Grated Parmigiano-Reggiano cheese

1 (16-ounce) bag frozen Trader Joe's Uncooked Wild Blue Shrimp, thawed

When you're short on time but need to whip up an impressive dish for a date, this is the one to turn to.

1. In a medium pot over medium-high heat, melt 1 tablespoon butter. Add the couscous, stirring to coat with butter.
2. Add the water to the couscous and season with salt and pepper. Bring the liquid to a boil, then cover the pot. Reduce the heat to low and cook until the couscous is tender, 10 to 12 minutes.
3. Meanwhile, in a small bowl, combine the lemon juice, oil, and cheese.
4. In a medium skillet over high heat, melt the remaining 1½ tablespoons butter. Add the shrimp and sauté until cooked and pink, 2 to 3 minutes. Remove from the heat and add the lemon sauce. Pour the shrimp and lemon sauce over the couscous, stirring to combine.

RAVIOLI *with* BROWN BUTTER SAUCE

YIELD: 4 servings
PREP TIME: 1 minute
COOKING TIME: 10 minutes

2 (9-ounce) packages Trader Giotto's Carbonara Stuffed Cheese Ravioli

5 tablespoons unsalted butter

1/3 (7-ounce) bag arugula

Brown butter is a rich, nutty sauce that's easy to prepare and makes you look like an ace in the kitchen.

1. Bring a medium pot of salted water to a boil over high heat. Cook the ravioli until al dente (see page 153), 4 to 6 minutes. Drain the pasta in a colander and set aside.
2. In a large saucepan over high heat, melt the butter, stirring constantly. Cook the butter until it gets frothy and turns a golden color, about 2 minutes. Remove from the heat.
3. Add the arugula, stirring until it wilts. Stir in the ravioli, coating it in the brown butter and arugula.

CHICKEN *with* 40 CLOVES *of* GARLIC

YIELD: 4 servings
PREP TIME: 5 minutes
COOKING TIME: 40 minutes

1 tablespoon canola oil

1 package Trader Joe's Organic Free Range Chicken Boneless Thighs (about 1½ pounds)

½ teaspoon kosher salt

¼ teaspoon freshly ground black pepper

1 cup chicken broth, or 1 cup hot water plus 1 (9.6-gram) pouch Trader Joe's Savory Chicken Concentrate

1 (4-ounce) bag Trader Joe's Premium Peeled Garlic

4 to 6 sprigs fresh thyme

This is one of my favorite recipes, and not just because it tastes like it took hours to prepare. Serve with crusty French bread to spread the soft garlic on.

1. Preheat the oven to 375°F.
2. In a large oven-safe pot, heat the oil over medium-high heat until shimmering.
3. Season the chicken thighs with salt and pepper and add them to pan. Sear briefly on each side until slightly golden in color, about 2 minutes per side.
4. Add the chicken broth, garlic, and thyme to the pot, stirring to combine. Remove from the heat and cover the pot.
5. Bake in the oven until the chicken thighs are done, 30 to 35 minutes. Cut into the thickest chicken piece to determine that it's no longer pink. Remove the thyme sprigs and serve the chicken with the garlic cloves and broth drizzled over the top.

WASABI-COATED CHICKEN

YIELD: 3 to 4 servings
PREP TIME: 15 minutes
COOKING TIME: 20 minutes

1½ cups Trader Joe-San Wasabi Peas

1 cup Trader Joe's Japanese-Style Panko Bread Crumbs

1 cup whole milk

1 large egg

kosher salt and freshly ground black pepper

1 pound Trader Joe's Organic Free Range Chicken Breast Tenders

kosher salt and freshly ground black pepper

canola oil, as needed

Pour a beer on the side and these greenish chicken tenders are fine fare for a St. Paddy's Day celebration.

1. Preheat the oven to 350°F.
2. Seal the wasabi peas into a plastic bag and pound them into crumbs. If you have a blender, you can also use that to crumble the peas. Place the crumbs in a medium bowl and mix in the panko bread crumbs.
3. In another medium bowl, use a fork or whisk to beat the milk and egg together to combine.
4. Season both sides of the chicken with salt and pepper. Dip each chicken tender into the milk-egg mixture and then into the wasabi-panko mixture.
5. In a medium skillet, heat 1 inch of oil over medium-high heat until shimmering. Add several chicken tenders (do not crowd the pan) and cook until the crust turns golden, about 1 minute per side. Remove the fried tenders to a rimmed baking sheet. Repeat until all the chicken tenders have been fried.
6. Transfer the baking sheet to the oven and bake until the chicken tenders are fully cooked, 6 to 8 minutes. Cut into the thickest chicken tender to determine it's no longer pink.
7. Remove from the oven and sprinkle with salt.

CHAPTER 11

DESSERTS & DRINKS

A lot of people sail through dinner just to make it to the dessert. I mean, who doesn't enjoy indulging in a sweet treat? When I was in college, my desserts consisted of dry cakes from the dining hall or a tub of Ben & Jerry's. Baking just wasn't something I did. Thinking back, it's pretty inexcusable. These recipes will reward you with some easy sugary decadence. There are tons of delicious homemade desserts that don't require a ton of work, like Sunflower Seed Butter Cookies, made from just three ingredients. And while some recipes, like Raspberry Brownies, are a great way to treat yourself at the end of the day, others, like Banana Bread with Pralines, are good for impressing your friends with your crazy baking skills.

And let's not forget about drinks. For some college students, drinking is mainly associated with the least expensive alcohol available. But, you can make boozy drinks that taste downright delicious, like sangria made from Trader Joe's affordable wines or a chocolate milkshake spiked with Kahlúa.

ULTIMATE BERRY MUFFINS

YIELD: 12 muffins
PREP TIME: 15 minutes
COOKING TIME: 25 minutes

2 cups water

1 (8-ounce) bag Trader Joe's Dried Berry Medley

2 large eggs

⅓ cup vegetable oil

1 (20-ounce) box Trader Joe's Cranberry Bread Mix

These can double as a breakfast snack or end-of-the-day treat.

1. Preheat the oven to 350°F. Spray 12 muffin cups with cooking spray.
2. Fill a microwave-safe bowl with the water, and microwave on high until the water boils, about 3 minutes. Add the dried berries to the water and let them soak for 10 minutes, then drain.
3. In a large bowl, use a fork or whisk to combine the eggs and oil. Add the cranberry bread mix and stir until the batter is combined. Gently fold in the berries with a spatula.
4. Fill each prepared muffin cup three-quarters full with batter. Bake until the tops of the muffins are crispy and a toothpick or knife inserted into the center comes out clean, 22 to 25 minutes.

SUNFLOWER SEED BUTTER COOKIES

YIELD: 12 cookies
PREP TIME: 10 minutes
COOKING TIME: 5 minutes

1 cup sugar

1 large egg

1 cup Trader Joe's Sunflower Seed Butter

This cookie recipe is for those days when you crave fresh, homemade cookies with little fuss.

1. Preheat the oven to 350°F. Spray a rimmed baking sheet with cooking spray.
2. In a medium bowl, mix the sugar, egg, and sunflower seed butter.
3. Roll tablespoons of dough into balls and arrange the balls about 1 inch apart on the prepared baking sheet.
4. Bake until just golden, about 5 minutes. Remove the cookies from the baking sheet onto waxed paper and let cool.

MONKEY BREAD

YIELD: 4 servings
PREP TIME: 15 minutes
COOKING TIME: 25 minutes

4 to 5 pieces Trader Joe's English Toffee with Milk Chocolate

⅓ cup unsalted butter, melted

2 (17.5-ounce) containers Trader Joe's Jumbo Cinnamon Rolls with Vanilla Icing

Monkey bread is a Southern staple. Balls of dough are rolled in cinnamon and sugar and drizzled with butter.

1. Preheat the oven to 350°F.
2. Seal the toffee into a plastic bag and pound into crumbs.
3. Drizzle the bottom of an 8-inch round pan with half of the butter and half of the crumbled toffee.
4. Unroll the cinnamon rolls and reserve the icing. Divide each one in half, then roll the halves into balls. Line up the cinnamon balls snugly next to each other in the pan. If you use a smaller pan, you may need to layer the balls on top of each other, which is fine. Drizzle the remaining butter over them and sprinkle with the remaining toffee crumbles.
5. Bake until bread is puffy and golden, about 25 minutes. Remove from the oven, and, if desired, drizzle the monkey bread with the reserved icing. Pull apart bread pieces to serve.

RASPBERRY BROWNIES

YIELD: 4 to 6 servings
PREP TIME: 10 minutes
COOKING TIME: 40 minutes

1 cup light sour cream

¼ cup applesauce

1 (13.7-ounce) box Trader Joe's Reduced Guilt (Fat-Free) Brownies

½ cup Trader Joe's Raspberry Preserves

If you're trying to ward off the Freshman 15 but still want to indulge in dessert, try these brownies that are on the low-fat side, made with applesauce instead of oil.

1. Preheat the oven to 350°F. Spray an 8-inch square pan with cooking spray.
2. In a large bowl, stir together the sour cream and applesauce. Add the brownie mix and stir until combined. Gently fold in the raspberry preserves with a spatula. Pour the batter into the prepared pan.
3. Bake until a knife or toothpick inserted into the center of the brownies comes out clean, 32 to 40 minutes.

BANANA BREAD *with* PRALINES

YIELD: 4 to 6 servings
PREP TIME: 10 minutes
COOKING TIME: 60 minutes

2 bananas, cut into pieces

2 large eggs

⅓ cup unsalted butter, melted

¾ cup water

1 (15-ounce) box Trader Joe's Banana Bread Mix

1 cup chopped Trader Joe's Pecan Pralines or Trader Joe's Candied Pecans

The addition of Trader Joe's Pecan Pralines really elevates this bread into the sublime.

1. Preheat the oven to 350°F. Spray a 9 x 5-inch loaf pan with cooking spray.
2. In a large bowl, mash the bananas with a fork.
3. In a medium bowl, whisk together the eggs, butter, and water. Pour the wet ingredients into the bananas, stirring to combine.
4. Add the banana bread mix to the wet ingredients and mix with a spatula until well combined. Fold in the pralines. Pour the batter into the prepared pan.
5. Bake until a toothpick or knife inserted into the center of the bread comes out clean, about 60 minutes.

VANILLA PUDDING CAKE

YIELD: 4 to 6 servings
PREP TIME: 20 minutes
COOKING TIME: 60 minutes

1 (16-ounce) box Trader Joe's Vanilla Cake and Baking Mix

1¾ cups milk, divided

½ cup vegetable oil

3 large eggs

2 tablespoons grated lemon zest, divided

1 (3.39-ounce) box Trader Joe's Instant Vanilla Pudding

This cake is poked with holes once it comes out of the oven—that's not a mistake. The pudding topping is then poured over it to soak into the cake.

1. Preheat the oven to 350°F. Spray an 8- or 9-inch round pan with cooking spray.
2. Pour the cake mix into a large bowl. Add ½ cup milk and the oil, eggs, and 1 tablespoon lemon zest. Mix the ingredients with a whisk until well combined. Pour the batter into the prepared pan.
3. Bake until the cake is golden and the center springs back when touched, 45 to 60 minutes.
4. In a microwave-safe dish, microwave the remaining 1¼ cups milk on high until warm, about 1½ minutes. Add the pudding mix, stirring until the pudding is thick. Stir in the remaining 1 tablespoon lemon zest.
5. Using a knife or chopstick, poke 15 to 20 holes in the cake. Slowly pour the hot pudding over the cake so it fills the holes and is absorbed by the cake. Let cool.

GINGER ICEBOX CAKE

YIELD: 4 servings
PREP TIME: 30 minutes active,
plus overnight to set up

1 tablespoon minced ginger

2 cups heavy cream, chilled

1 tablespoon sugar

2 (9-ounce) packages
Trader Joe's Cookie Thins Triple
Ginger cookies

Icebox cakes are the easiest no-bake cakes ever.

1. In a large bowl, place the ginger, cream, and sugar. Using an electric handheld mixer on high speed, beat the cream until stiff peaks form, 2 to 3 minutes, to make ginger-flavored whipped cream.

2. Set aside about one-fifth of the whipped cream and 6 cookies. On a large plate, use a spatula to gently spread about 2 tablespoons of the whipped cream to hold the bottom layer of cookies to the plate. Fit as many cookies as you can in a single layer on the plate.

3. On top of the cookies, spread a thin layer of whipped cream with a spatula. Repeat, adding another layer of cookies and whipped cream. Continue layering the cookies and whipped cream until you have 8 to 10 layers.

4. Use a spatula to cover the top and sides of the cake with the reserved whipped cream. Cover with plastic wrap and refrigerate for at least 8 hours.

5. When you're ready to serve the cake, seal the 6 reserved cookies into a plastic bag and pound into crumbles. Sprinkle the top of the cake with the crumbles.

NUTTY CARAMEL POPCORN

YIELD: 4 servings
PREP TIME: 5 minutes
COOKING TIME: 5 minutes

1 (3.2-ounce) packet Trader Joe's Microwave Popcorn with Natural Popcorn Flavor

3 tablespoons unsalted butter, melted

1 cup Trader Jacques' Fleur de Sel Caramel Sauce

1 cup Trader Joe's Roasted and Salted Mixed Nuts

In addition to giving you a very brief French lesson, the fleur de sel (artisinal salt) in the caramel sauce helps bring out the saltiness of the popcorn.

1. Microwave the popcorn according to the package directions. Set aside.
2. In a large bowl, stir together the melted butter and caramel sauce to combine. Pour half of the popcorn into the bowl, along with the nuts. Stir to combine, making sure to coat all the popcorn with the caramel on the bottom of the bowl. Add the remaining popcorn and continue stirring to coat with the caramel.
3. Spread the popcorn mixture onto a baking sheet. Let sit for 5 to 10 minutes to slightly harden.

CHOCOLATE FONDUE

YIELD: 4 servings
PREP TIME: 5 minutes
COOKING TIME: 2 minutes

2 bananas

½ Trader Joe's Angel Food Cake

1 (1.2-ounce) package Trader Joe's Freeze Dried Strawberries

½ cup Trader Joe's Organic Midnight Moo Chocolate Flavored Syrup

½ cup semisweet chocolate chips, divided

This fondue is so quick and easy to make using Trader Joe's chocolate syrup.

1. Cut the bananas and the cake into bite-size pieces. Arrange them on a plate, along with the dried strawberries.
2. In a small microwave-safe bowl, stir together the chocolate syrup and ¼ cup chocolate chips. Microwave on high until melted, 1 to 1½ minutes.
3. Remove from the microwave and stir in the remaining ¼ cup chocolate chips.
4. Serve, dipping the fruit and cake pieces into the fondue. Reheat the fondue for 10 to 20 seconds in the microwave if it cools down.

DIRT DESSERT

YIELD: 10 servings
PREP TIME: 30 minutes

1 (20-ounce) box Joe-Joe's
Chocolate Sandwich
Creme Cookies

3 cups milk

2 (4.09-ounce) boxes Trader Joe's
Instant Chocolate Pudding

2 tablespoons unsalted butter,
softened

8 ounces cream cheese, softened

1 cup powdered sugar

1 can sweetened light
whipped cream

This is a simple dessert that requires no actual baking and always draws rave reviews. It's a delicious, ultrarich chocolate mess.

1. Seal the cookies into a large plastic bag and pound to a sandlike consistency with a rolling pin or the bottom of a pan.

2. In a medium bowl, whisk together the milk and pudding mix until the pudding thickens. Set aside.

3. In a large bowl, place the butter, cream cheese, and sugar. Using an electric handheld mixer on low speed, cream the mixture until well combined and fluffy, 2 to 3 minutes. If you don't have a mixer, use a spoon, but make sure to mix it well. Using a spatula, fold the reserved chocolate pudding into the cream cheese mixture. Spray the whipped cream into the bowl, and fold in to combine.

4. In a large serving bowl, spread one-third of the chocolate mixture, then one-third of the cookie crumbs. Repeat 2 times.

Note: The appearance of the top layer of cookie crumbs makes the dish look like a big bowl of dirt—if you want to get cute, you can place some gummy worms so that they look like they're crawling out of the top.

SPIKED CHOCOLATE MILKSHAKE

YIELD: 2 servings
PREP TIME: 5 minutes

1 cup Trader Joe's Ultra Chocolate Ice Cream

5 Joe-Joe's Chocolate Sandwich Creme Cookies (any variety), plus 2 for garnish

¾ cup Kahlúa, or other coffee liqueur

canned sweetened light whipped cream (optional)

These milkshakes may look on the small side, but they're very rich.

1. In a blender, place the ice cream, cookies, and Kahlúa. (Use more or less ice cream if you prefer a thicker or thinner shake). Blend on high until combined.

2. Pour the milkshakes into 2 glasses. Top with whipped cream, if desired, and garnish with the remaining cookies crumbled on top.

BOURBON STREET SHAKE

YIELD: 2 servings
PREP TIME: 5 minutes

1 cup Trader Joe's French Vanilla Ice Cream

1 tablespoon Trader Jacques' Fleur de Sel Caramel Sauce

⅓ cup whole milk

⅓ cup bourbon

Vanilla ice cream and bourbon meet a touch of salted caramel in this dreamy shake.

1. In a blender, place the ice cream, caramel sauce, milk, and bourbon. (Use more or less ice cream if you prefer a thicker or thinner shake). Blend on high until combined.

2. Pour the milkshakes into 2 glasses.

MICHELADA

YIELD: 1 serving
PREP TIME: 5 minutes

This is a riff on the popular Tex-Mex version of a refreshing summer beer.

ice

2 tablespoons tomato juice

juice of 1 lime

½ teaspoon Trader Joe's Jalapeño Pepper Hot Sauce, or more

1 (12-ounce) bottle Trader José Premium Lager

1. Fill a large glass with ice.
2. Pour in the tomato juice, lime juice, and hot sauce, and stir to combine.
3. Slowly pour in the beer. Gently stir.

LOVE DRUNK PUNCH

YIELD: 6 to 8 servings
PREP TIME: 5 minutes

The sparkling cider gives this punch an invigorating fizziness. Try not to make it too far in advance, as the carbonation will gradually fade.

½ (12-ounce) can frozen Trader Joe's Organic Orange Juice, thawed

2 cups Trader Joe's 100% Pineapple Juice

1½ cups rum

½ cup peach liqueur

4 cups Trader Joe's Sparkling Apple Cider

1. In a large pitcher or bowl, place the orange juice, pineapple juice, rum, and peach liqueur. Stir or shake to combine, making sure the orange juice is dissolved.
2. Add the sparking apple cider, stirring more to combine.

SANGRIA

YIELD: 4 servings
PREP TIME: 5 minutes

1 (25-ounce) jar Trader Joe's Pear Halves in White Grape Juice

1 (750 ml) bottle La Ferme Julien Rosé, or any other rosé or dry red wine

¼ cup triple sec

1 cup seltzer water

1 orange, cut into wedges

1 lemon, cut into wedges

1 bunch red grapes

Sangria is a blend of wine, juice, and chunks of citrus or other fresh fruit.

1. Chop the pears into small chunks and reserve the juice.

2. In a pitcher, stir together the grape juice from the pears, the wine, triple sec, and seltzer water.

3. Add the pear slices, orange wedges, lemon wedges, and grapes.

4. Refrigerate for a few hours until chilled.

GINGER BEER LEMONADE

YIELD: 4 servings
PREP TIME: 5 minutes

5 to 6 lemons

⅓ cup sugar

2 cups water

2 (12-ounce) bottles Reed's Ginger Beer

If you haven't discovered the deliciousness that is Reed's Ginger Beer, available at Trader Joe's, then let this serve as an excuse to try it.

1. Juice the lemons into a large pitcher.

2. Add the sugar, stirring to combine. Add the water, stirring to combine.

3. Top with the ginger beer, stirring to combine.

TIPS & TECHNIQUES

HOW TO PREPARE AN AVOCADO

Use a chef's knife to carefully cut the avocado lengthwise around the seed, cutting all the way through to the seed. Stab the seed with the knife, then twist and remove. To dice the avocado, take one half in your hand and use a paring knife to cut a crosshatch pattern into the avocado without going through to the peel. To slice, cut lengthwise. Use a large spoon and scoop out the avocado dice or slices.

HOW TO DICE AN ONION

1. Cut the onion in half vertically, straight through the root end and the stem end.
2. Peel both halves of the onion, discarding the peel.
3. Place the halves on a cutting board, cut-side down. Trim the stem ends.
4. Make numerous parallel cuts from the root end to the stem end, making sure to keep the root end intact. Cuts that are farther apart will result in larger dice; cuts closer together will yield smaller dice.
5. Carefully hold the onion at the root end. Make two or more even horizontal cuts, holding your knife parallel to the cutting board.
6. Holding the root end, slice crosswise, starting at the opposite end. The onion will fall into dice.

HOW TO BOIL AN EGG

If Trader Joe's is out of hard-cooked peeled eggs, or you just want to know how to make hard-cooked eggs on your own, here's what to do: In a medium pot, cover 6 to 8 large eggs with enough water to cover them. Bring the water to a boil over high heat. As soon as the water comes to a full rolling boil, cover the pot with a lid and remove it from the heat. Let the eggs sit in the hot water for 12 minutes. Carefully drain the hot water from the eggs. Fill the pot with cold water and ice cubes until the eggs have cooled enough to peel. For easiest and neatest peeling, do it as soon as possible.

HOW TO COOK AL DENTE PASTA

When cooking pasta, the goal is to boil it until it's al dente. But what exactly does that mean? An Italian phrase meaning "to the bite," al dente refers to the point when the pasta is cooked but still slightly firm to the bite. The best way to determine this is to taste the pasta as it cooks. Also, immediately after draining the pasta in a colander, make sure to toss it with a little olive oil. This prevents the pasta strands from sticking to each other and making a glop of noodles.

COOKING STEAK AND BURGERS

Keep in mind that the internal temperature of meat will rise by about 5 degrees while resting and that the following guidelines for beef account for that: for rare, 120° to 125°F; for medium-rare, 130° to 140°F; for medium, 145° to 150°F; for well-done, 155° to 165°F. The most accurate way to determine the doneness of steak is by using a meat thermometer, but you'll lose a bit of juice when the thermometer pokes a hole into the steak.

With a little of practice, you can learn to determine doneness by merely touching the steak with your finger—rare steak feels soft, with a lot of give; a tiny more give yields medium-rare; medium steak yields only slightly to the touch; and well-done steak feels hard to the touch. Resting is important because it allows the steak to finish cooking and retain its juiciness by redistributing its juices. If you cut into a steak without letting it rest, lots of delicious juices will escape.

IDEAS FOR LEFTOVER TRADER JOE'S INGREDIENTS

PESTO

- Whisk with vinegar and olive oil to make salad dressing.

- Mix with sour cream and dollop onto a baked potato or stir into mashed potatoes.

- Smear onto chicken, top with bread crumbs, and bake.

- Swirl into tomato soup.

- Beat into eggs before scrambling.

- Add 1 or 2 tablespoons to cooked rice, polenta, or grits.

- Dilute with oil and use as a marinade for meat.

- Layer onto a grilled cheese sandwich.

- Toss with ½ pound cooked Trader Joe's Italian Capellini pasta and Trader Joe's Grilled Lemon Pepper Chicken.

ALMOND BUTTER AND BANANA SANDWICH

Wanna make this sandwich à la Elvis? Melt a little butter in a nonstick skillet over medium-high heat and sauté the assembled sandwich on each side until golden. Sprinkle with powdered sugar and serve.

PINE NUTS

Pine nuts are the edible seeds from certain varieties of pine trees. The small, almond-shaped nuts are actually located inside the pine cone. It's a time-consuming process to remove the nuts from the cones, which explains why pine nuts can be priced higher than other nuts. Add leftover pine nuts to any dish like soups, salads, and pastas when you want a touch of crunchiness.

RAW SHRIMP

Large, raw shrimp (peeled and deveined), like Trader Joe's Uncooked Wild Blue Shrimp, can be used instead of the cooked shrimp if you want a fresher taste. Thaw the shrimp, then cook as directed, increasing the time to 2 minutes.

CHILI

Use the leftover chili and queso dip to replace the chili and sour cream in a Frito Pie (page 18). Or, pour it over tortilla chips for nachos, or use it to top a burger.

CONVERSIONS

MEASURE	EQUIVALENT	METRIC
1 teaspoon		5.0 milliliters
1 tablespoon	3 teaspoons	14.8 milliliters
1 cup	16 tablespoons	236.8 milliliters
1 pint	2 cups	473.6 milliliters
1 quart	4 cups	947.2 milliliters
1 liter	4 cups + 3½ tablespoons	1000 milliliters
1 ounce (dry)	2 tablespoons	28.35 grams
1 pound	16 ounces	453.49 grams
2.21 pounds	35.3 ounces	1 kilogram
350°F / 400°F		175°C / 200°C

PHOTO CREDITS

Images are credited on their first appearance in the book.

p. 3: © Judi Swinks

p. 5: © marinamik/fotolia.com

p. 6: microwave © Agb/fotolia.com

p. 6: pot © Daevid/fotolia.com

p. 6: timer © Agb/fotolia.com

p. 6: stove © Agb/fotolia.com

p. 6: backpack © Manish/fotolia.com

p. 6: radish © Agb/fotolia.com

p. 9: © martinlee/fotolia.com

p. 10: © Judi Swinks

p. 15: © Judi Swinks

p. 17: © Dušan Zidar/fotolia.com

p. 19: © Judi Swinks

p. 23: © Daniel Wiedemann/fotolia.com

p. 25: © Judi Swinks

p. 27: © Paul Cowan/fotolia.com

p. 28: © Judi Swinks

p. 31: © mark huls/fotolia.com

p. 32: © Yasonya/fotolia.com

p. 34: © Judi Swinks

p. 38: © Judi Swinks

p. 41: © Elena Schweitzer/fotolia.com

p. 42: © eAlisa/fotolia.com

p. 45: © Judi Swinks

p. 47: © Norman Chan/fotolia.com

p. 50: © Judi Swinks

p. 55: © Judi Swinks

p. 57: © Marc Dietrich/fotolia.com

p. 59: © Leonid Nyshko/fotolia.com

p. 60: © Judi Swinks

p. 63: © Judi Swinks

p. 64: © unknown1861/fotolia.com

p. 65: © Doris Rich/shutterstock.com

p. 66: © Judi Swinks

p. 70: © Judi Swinks

p. 72: © volff/fotolia.com

p. 73: © Dionisvera/fotolia.com

p. 75: © Picture Partners/fotolia.com

p. 77: © Judi Swinks

p. 79: © greenfire/fotolia.com

p. 83: © Judi Swinks

p. 84: © philipus/fotolia.com

p. 86: © scol22/fotolia.com

p. 89: © Judi Swinks

p. 93: © Judi Swinks

p. 95: © Christian Jung/fotolia.com

p. 96: © Judi Swinks

p. 99: © Judi Swinks

p. 100: © Franco Deriu/fotolia.com

p. 102: © fafoutis/fotolia.com

p. 105: © Tomboy2290/fotolia.com

p. 107: © Judi Swinks

p. 108: © Brett Mulcahy/fotolia.com

p. 110: © Judi Swinks

p. 113: © Judi Swinks

p. 115: © felix/fotolia.com

p. 118: © Judi Swinks

p. 123: © Judi Swinks

p. 125: © marilyn barbone/fotolia.com

p. 127: © Judi Swinks

p. 131: © Judi Swinks

p. 133: © Tomboy2290/fotolia.com

p. 135: © Judi Swinks

p. 136: © ALEXANDRA/fotolia.com

p. 139: © Doris Rich/shutterstock.com

p. 143: © Judi Swinks

p. 147: © Judi Swinks

p. 152: © eyewave/fotolia.com

RECIPE INDEX

ABOUT THE AUTHOR

ANDREA LYNN, author of *Fresh and Healthy DASH Diet Cooking* and *The Artisan Soda Workshop*, is a food writer and recipe developer with a culinary arts degree from the Institute of Culinary Education and a creative writing degree from Agnes Scott College. She has worked as a personal chef and as senior editor at *Chile Pepper* magazine. Her articles and recipes have appeared in print and online for numerous publications. Andrea has tasted almost every product Trader Joe's has on the market.